Published by Borland Ceilidh Press

Kilmarnock

www.borlandceilidhband.com

ISBN: 978-0-244-21991-8

Designed and typeset by Borland Ceilidh Press

Cover design © Paul Kerr

'I would also like to say a thank you to the Music legend that is Jamie Cullum for his Song 'All At Sea' this song helped me through a tough time and his talents deserve my public acknowledgement'

To contact the author: -

paulalexanderkerr1@gmail.com

Version: September 20, 2019 10:18 PM

Thanks

When my family friend Jane suggested that my experiences in life were of value to others, and that there was a book in my past, I laughed at the thought. What could a dyslexic former Royal Marine Commando, who had been diagnosed seven years ago with a very serious illness, have to say that others would want to read?

Thinking further about it, I realised, well yes, when I was first diagnosed I would have loved to have read about someone in my situation, and to know what they had done in spite of it.

I have a strong set of life skills from my time as a Commando, as well as values that have helped me live with my condition. These skills and values have helped me through my journey so far and my aim now is to pass the benefits of my experiences to my readers, and to share how my thoughts have helped, and hindered, along the way.

I can prove to you that there is no need to lose faith in yourself; and that your situation can be improved. A good mind set is more likely to lead to good outcomes. Whether you're feeling negative or positive does make a difference to your situation.

Trust me; your thoughts fuel fires.

I hope you enjoy my book and that you are able to find some-thing here that seems just right for you. And remember

tomorrow is another day

Paul A Kerr

Chapters

Foreword

Multiple sclerosis is the commonest chronic nerve disorder that occurs in young adults. It is characterised by progressive disability. The features of the disease include weakness, sensory disturbance, pain, and impairment of balance.

Paul's book tells the story of the impact of the diagnosis of Multiple Sclerosis on a young fit man. It chronicles his determination to realise his potential in life by utilising his personal strengths and drawing on the ethos of 'smiling through adversity' that was instilled during his training as a Royal Marines Commando.

I hope that his book will serve as an inspiration to all, but in particular to those who are challenged by multiple sclerosis or other chronic disease in early adult life.

Sir Ranulph Fiennes

Acknowledgements

In my life I owe many people considerable thanks! But to make my book into a reality it took a lot of help and time from a number of people. I would like to mention there having been time and valued input from: -

Dr Sheila Cameron

Georgia Love

Colin Cameron

John Grant

Without the help of these people my book would have stayed no more than a dream.

Never give up ... never lose heart

Chapter 1 – This Is Me Now, (2015)!

I organise and take part in a swim across the River Clyde every year; and to help you understand the book going forward I'm going to go take you to June 23rd, 2012.

I was having a glass of wine with my father and Tom Brannan one evening at my parents' house. The conversation was about what my next physical challenge was going to be, as it was a couple of years since I had done 'The Three Peaks Challenge' (more about that later on), and they knew I would have been making a plan of some sort.

I thought about this as the wine flowed and then spoke of a challenge that had been in my thoughts since I was very young, and something that I had discussed with friends over the years. I knew that if I chose to do this there would be a number of kindred spirits who would step up to it with me. I decided I would swim across the River Clyde.

The beauty of coming up with this challenge on this evening was that Tom owns a couple of maritime companies on the Clyde: Shearwater Marine and The Professional Diving Academy. He also had a number of boats as well as staff who could help with safety. A good number of his staff are also my friends and I knew they would be keen to get in the water with me.

I started with putting a few feelers out to my mates who did the Three Peaks with me to see who was up for it, and also ask if the idea was mad. What was coming to light was, yes it was mad, but my friends being my friends, the fact that they thought it was mad is what caught their attention.

I did some research on open water swimming style and the stroke best to use, and it became apparent that I would be best to do the front crawl. It was a stroke I could do, but the problem was I had never had to do it over long distance.

I looked out my windsurfing wetsuit from my parents' basement. It hadn't seen water for a good few years, and that had been when I last went windsurfing. I went down to Toward Sailing Club to get back in the water. It had been a few years since I had gone in, but the water was calm and there were no boats out, so it was safe. I had an old diver's hood to wear too, which was also from my windsurfing days. It's funny, I was looking at these things from my past, realising that I had thought I would never use them again; yet here I was finding new uses for them.

For open swimming over distance you are always looking for a transit to head for, and for me front crawl was best, but I needed to work on my endurance with this. You need to think about the other water users, your location tides, and you always have to have contingencies; the list goes on and on, so it's not something to do without a lot of different kinds of knowledge.

The people closest to me were really encouraged that I was

deciding to take this challenge on. Yes sure, they maybe thought I was slightly mad and certainly a touch eccentric, but that I also needed this in my life at that time.

Ok, I admit it; I had got the tide times slightly wrong on that first Clyde swim back on June 23rd, 2012. I'm sorry about that everyone, but I think you will find it was me who was washed the furthest away from the finish line. We've got it right every year since, but admittedly there is a proper team to run it now - led from the front by Lorn Campbell.

In year one I actually ended upstream, heading north and towards Glasgow by about a mile from where I had planned the finish to be at the Rock Cafe at the foot of Castle Hill in Dunoon. I ended up landing just across from my church, Saint Munn's, when I made it to the shore. So I might not have made the finish line, but the way I saw it was that I had made it across the Clyde; something I had wanted to do my whole life, and I had finally achieved it.

My parents were with my then partner Sarah and my son Zander in the safety boat the whole way across. I did front crawl the whole way and could intermittently hear Zander's shouts of encouragement as I came up for my breaths of air between strokes.

Tom Brannan was the skipper of the boat they were in. I had already discussed with Tom that he would be my marker and

I would rely on him to keep me going in the right direction. Swimming in the sea is very different to a pool; there is no blue line to follow on the bottom, no wall to push off every 25 metres, and nothing close by giving you the obvious feel of progression. It's a real test of your mental endurance and tenacity.

It was an emotional day. For me, it was a success even to get out of the boat at the Cloch Lighthouse and into the water to begin the swim back to Dunoon. The plan was actually coming together; I was finally swimming across the Clyde with five-year-old Zander at my side in the safety boat shouting: "Nearly there Dad! Only two more miles to go!" And as for my parents, what they must have been feeling is beyond me.

After a couple hours of non-stop front crawl and looking at the freeboard (the part of a boat from the water line up to the deck) of Tom's boat, The The Synolda, the whole way, I finally made it to the other side. Yes, it was a mile upstream from where I had planned and had told the other 16 swimmers to head for, but it was the other side of the Clyde!

Funnily enough, when I was crawling up the beach feeling very pleased with myself I noticed, no more than 10 metres away from me, my close friend Ewen Munro also crawling. He clocked me at the same time and the pair of us let out a yell of surprised delight at seeing each other. It dawned on us that we had been right next to each other the whole way over. Ewen had also done the Three Peaks Mountain Challenge with me a couple of years before, and so had a few of the others swimming the Clyde that day, but they had been more successful in reaching the planned end point.

I still had a key part of the day to come though, and it was in my mind the whole way over. Zander is an amazing swimmer, and had been training hard in the pool with me the past few months. He had asked for a wetsuit and if he could please join me in the water for the final 25 metres.

So I got back in the water and swam out to The Synolda and climbed in it with Zander, Sarah and my parents. I remember seeing my mother's look of pride, and remembered that I had seen that look many years before at Lympstone Commando when getting my Green Beret.

Zander was in his wetsuit and ready to take the plunge. It's such a big deal to a wee guy; the open sea is not the pool. It's daunting and can really test a person's mettle. Once in the boat we headed round to the planned finish point of the West Bay. As we approached, I was amazed to see hundreds of people lined up on the shore. The local paper reported that there was a crowd of around 200 people to welcome us.

Tom positioned The Synolda 25 metres from the shore and I jumped off her stern so that I was in the water ready to support Zander for his own Clyde Challenge. Tom momentarily killed the engine and Zander jumped off, and from there we swam towards the very supportive Dunoon crowd waiting to greet us with hot soup and pats on the back.

From that day, The Clyde Charity Challenge has gone from strength to strength in both numbers and organisation. It is now a recognised day in Dunoon's calendar with 60 places a year, and with people travelling for it from as far as Thailand and Germany. When it suits, I take part myself.

As I stood on the shore, happy and proud that I had achieved another life-long dream as well as undergoing a gruelling physical challenge, I reflected that it had not always been like this, and that I had gone through some very dark days indeed - and only a few years before.

Post Clyde swim soup from my big sister Nicola

Chapter 2 – Schoolboy To Bootneck (Born To 1997)

It's safe to say I had quite a privileged upbringing. I was brought up in the small town of Dunoon in Argyll on the west coast of Scotland, and my earlier life was like a cross between the films 'The Goonies' and 'Stand By Me'.

Life was packed with safe, secure, but adventurous fun. My weekends were spent either playing soldiers in the hills behind my house or in one of the local forests, building tree houses with friends. There was also a long stretch of beach in front of my house where we would make boats out of whatever had been washed up. I didn't know it at the time but these experiences were already moulding me and would stay with me in my adult life.

The River Clyde is a vibrant stretch of water with a lot going on, and there was a lot of military excitement for a young lad to look out at. Faslane Naval Base was literally only a few miles away, so submarines were an everyday sight, as well as fishing boats, ferries, and merchant shipping. Dunoon was also the home for decades to the US Navy at their base at Holy Loch on the Clyde. We also had the excitement of fighter jets and Hercules planes flying over the house some evenings on exercise. You get the idea - there was quite a varied military presence from my earliest years.

Mum and Dad were childhood sweethearts, and they brought

up my sister Nicola and me with not a lot of money, but certainly a lot of love. After Dad retired from the Glasgow police, he and Mum were looking for a quieter life for their young family. I was only three years old at the time, and that period is more of a dreamy haze to me. So, although it was a large chapter in my parents' lives, to me it's more like a dimly remembered page in a book that you once flicked through.

When it comes to school, I have quite varied emotions. At the time I thought it was tough, but as it makes me laugh looking back now, I can't say for sure if my memories are in truth good or bad. School was just school. It was something that you had no choice in; it just had to be dealt with by going. Because where I lived was quiet, I would safely walk to school in the morning passing friends' houses, as well as a number of bramble bushes, so at certain times of the year actually getting us to school on time and without our white school shirts covered in dark purple bramble juice was quite a feat for our parents.

I look back on my earlier school years and remember being nervous and rather insecure, but in all honesty I was probably no more so than the other kids my age. What I was noticing, though, was that some of the kids in my class could read far better than me, and although I was very good at figuring out sums in my head I was not so good at putting them down on paper. I had always been rubbish at football, but that didn't concern me as it was never something I was drawn to anyway.

Bikes and skateboards had always been my thing.

We lived along the road from a fish farm in the village of Toward called Murray Sea Foods. I remember it well. I had always been quite big for my age, and now I was 12 years old, my insecurities were passing and I decided that I was ready to earn some serious pocket money. So I got on my bike and cycled to the fish farm, went into the main office and nervously stuttered: "My name's Paul Kerr, and is there any weekend work please Miss?"

To my amazement, the lady in the office started to ask questions and take notes so she could ask the boss. The problem was I hadn't planned this far ahead.

When she asked: "How old are you, Paul, and when can you start?" I quickly became 16 (in reality only 12) and able to start on Saturday. I soon became the wealthiest 12-year-old in school. I learned what it was like to go to work at 6am on a Saturday morning, and what it's also like to be wet and cold for the day if you don't have your personal admin 'squared away' (Marine talk for your essential life requirements). Once you left the work shed in the morning and the boat had slipped the pier to go offshore to work on the cages at sea, then tough luck, Paul. Looking back now I can see how these were all good life lessons.

The years passed, and before I knew it I actually was 16 years old and no stranger to waking up at 5am on a Saturday morning. Lying in bed listening to the fabulous Scottish winters hammering my bedroom window, the new BMX didn't seem quite so attractive on those mornings but I could never let my colleagues down. I wouldn't have liked that myself, and also Big H would have given me a right hiding the following weekend. Hilariously, Big H ended up following in my footsteps and also ended up joining the Royal Marines.

Winters were long, dark and cold, and summers were very smelly with jellyfish to sting you at every opportunity, and to add to that the seaweed would grow on the cage nets far quicker, so everything was more slippery and heavier.

So here I was, working at the fish farm more and more, while my school grades were never going to get me into university, and I couldn't see myself heading to college. But fish farm life was not a long term plan either.

One day, while out feeding the fish, a couple of super cool military fast assault craft came flying past the farm cage I was working on. They were full of combat-dressed soldiers on an exercise, and I later found out after some research that they were Royal Marine Commandos.

It turned out they were from Commachio Group, the Royal Marine unit based at Faslane. After seeing these boats I phoned up the careers office in Glasgow and had my first entrance interview the following week.

Chapter 3 – Green Beret (1997 To 2003)

I started my Basic Training for the Royal Marines the following month, and nine months later was awarded my coveted Green Beret. I was also drafted up to FPGRM at Faslane, the very unit of men that inspired me to join the Corps in the first place.

This was an incredible time in my life and a vital juncture for me, a young lad who had no real experience of the world, other than school and fish farming.

After a gruelling nine month course at the Commando Training Centre of the Royal Marines (CTCRM) where I was taken, both mentally and physically, to the edge on the world-renowned Commando course. Finally here I was, standing in the prestigious Falklands Hall waiting for the curtain to go back and for my parents to see me for the first time in months, and to witness me being awarded my Green Beret.

I can still remember standing in Troop Formation behind the curtain and hearing Major Buster Howes (now Major General Buster Howes and one of the most impressive men I've been fortunate to meet) saying to the room of parents and families: "Ladies and gentlemen, it is my honour to introduce to you The King Squad." He was referring to us, at the end of training and about to start our career in the world-respected Royal Marines.

The curtain then went back, slowly. You are not allowed to

move a muscle when on important parade like this. It's an example of your excellence and personal discipline, but your eyes will certainly scan the room. So, standing rigidly to attention and looking through the room of parents, I finally found mine clapping furiously and sitting on the edge of their seats, bursting with pride and smiling from ear to ear.

I chose to spend only six years in the Marines. I remember why I decided to leave. I had been drafted out to spend a year in the Indian Ocean on the island of Diego Garcia doing ship boardings in the wake of the attack on the Twin Towers on September 11th, 2001.

While there, I was offered a job if I chose to leave the Corps after my Diego Garcia draft. I'd be working on a ship out of the island of South Georgia doing fisheries protection in the South Atlantic. This opportunity seemed too good an experience to pass up, and the pay was not too shabby either, so I naturally jumped at this and my next big life experience began. However, I loved the Corps; I still do, and I miss it and the lads every day.

Postcard from Poland

Chapter 4 – South Georgia (Towards The End Of 2003)

I was only offered this South Georgia opportunity because I had been in the Marines, and because at this point in my life I had proven I had self-control, a 'can do' attitude and had, more importantly, proved I can smile in the face of adversity.

After a long journey down to Puntarenas with stop-offs in Madrid and a night in the airport at Santiago in Chile, I walked out looking for my contact who was to sort me out locally while I was there. My lift from the airport was in the back of a pickup truck with maybe 15 other men on their way to work. It's safe to say it was a very different place to back home, but I was enjoying the relaxedness of it. I was so far south that it was starting to get cold; dry but cold, so the back of the flat bed pickup was a cold lift.

Thankfully I finally met my ship, 'The Isla Camila'. She was getting old, older than I was, and she looked like she needed a good coat of paint, but she was my home for the next four months and the place where I would learn a lot about myself as a person.

So I went aboard her and met the crew and the officers; a good bunch of men and I had faith in their confidence. It wasn't their first time down there and they were keen to get going, so this told me enough to relax about what was going to happen.

I had been advised to learn Spanish, and at the time this didn't seem too big a deal, as I was now quite cognisant with the Boot-neck (Marine) standard in life of 'No cuff too tough' - ie the personal belief and knowledge that you really can do anything if you have the guts to try and the tenacity to see it through.

Looking back at this it was a daunting time, as not knowing too much about a situation can be terrifying. Think about this - I was to be on a boat with crew I knew nothing about, in very big seas and with little outside support. If something went wrong here with the vessel, it would happen fast and help would have been slow to reach us, because we were in a very remote part of the world, with men whose language I didn't speak, and neither did they speak mine.

Heading down to South Georgia on a 47 metre boat with 43 Chilean Spanish-speaking crew was certainly daunting. Strangely, my main concern though was potential toothache. What will I do if I get toothache? How will I deal with it? I always like to have a contingency plan, and my initial thought was: 'I have my Bootneck Leatherman (a combi tool) and I'll just pull out the tooth in question if needed.' I then remem-bered that, in the past when I had toothache and would go to the dentist to have it sorted, Nigel my dentist would often work on a different tooth to the one I had thought was the problem. How would I know I was pulling on the right tooth? I had images of unbearable toothache, putting myself through the trauma of pulling my own tooth out only to discover once it was out it was the wrong tooth.

Once I had assuaged my toothache concern with a can of Coke and a Mars Bar, I read the book about Ernest Shackleton's epic journey 'Endurance', and I knew that we were landing on South Georgia just next to the obsolete but globally renowned Gritviking whaling station. I had read the legend that Sir Ernest was buried close by, so I was hoping to see his grave and pay my respects if possible.

After a couple of days on board The Isla Camila, sitting in a port in Puntarenas, we finally set sail and started our long voyage south where the boat would be working 24 hours a day for four months solid.

The type of fishing my boat was to be doing was called 'long lining', where it would run a fishing line out for maybe up to 11 kilometres. On the fishing line, every 100 metres, say, there was a hook with bait on it. Our boat would run the line and then come back to it a couple of days later and reel it back in I would immediately document its catch of Patagonian Tooth Fish, before the crew put the catch into deep freeze. As this part of the world is so untouched by direct human influence, I was there to ensure that the vessel was staying within the environmental demands put in place by CAMLAR (Commission for the Conservation of Antarctic Marine Living Resources). The situation was that, in effect, I was looking over and recording every detail of what The Isla Camila crew was doing and then reporting it back to headquarters on South Georgia.

This involved me going out on deck and looking over the long line as it came on board, sometimes sitting for up to three hours in -30 degree centigrade weather. I was there to ensure the waters around South Georgia were not mistreated or over-fished by my vessel - which they weren't, I might add.

This, however, did lead to me becoming rather paranoid at times, thinking the crew thought I was spying on them, but this was only due to my own imagination and nothing they did led to my paranoia.

I had read during my deployment study that the seas down around South Georgia have been recorded at being so large that from one wave to the next the tips can be up to one mile apart. I can vouch for this, but getting comfy with this lifestyle and learning to make it my normality has stood me in good stead in these recent years with vertigo.

The days went by, and so did the weeks and in due course the months. I became quite relaxed and able to sleep in South Georgia Seas that were so rough I would be crumpled up at one end of my bunk and then slide down to the other end straight after. I fell into the habit of speaking on the radio in the eve-nings with South Georgia scientists, and one in particular. It became bit of a must with me.

There was a female voice on the radio which became like a

drug to me, and the more time went by, the more I relied on hearing this voice to keep me sane and relatively relaxed in the evenings. At the end of the four months at sea at South Georgia, I did manage to get ashore and spend time with this girl; it was like a four-month dream come true…

I did also get to see Sir Ernest Shackleton's grave. It was from a distance, but still close enough for me to pay this legendary man my respects. I think that reading up on people like Sir Ernest Shacklelton and Sir Ranulph Feinnes has played a very big part in finding my own drive and strengths when times get hard. Their stories are educational and inspirational.

Anyway, I made it home safely after four long months of icebergs, killer whales, very rough seas and no-one to talk to as there were no phones on board in those days. If I'm honest, I made a poor effort regarding the standard of work and the reports I handed in. And between not speaking the language and having never been to university to study the required subject, I really had bitten off a large mouthful. But hey, onwards and upwards.

Me on the MV Isla Camila holding a couple of Patagonian Tooth fish down at at South Georgia

Chapter 5 – Civvy Street (2003/2004)

I finally arrived back in the UK after my time at sea. I had been sitting on a plane, stuck on the runway at Heathrow because the crew had decided to go on strike. The reality of Civvy Street was slowly settling in and it was also starting to dawn on me that, for the first time since walking into the office of Murray Sea Foods, I was going to have to go out and look for a job. Up until that moment I had been really fortunate with work finding me - right place, right time, I suppose.

I have always been the annoying type who sparks up a point-less conversation with whoever I happen to be sitting across from on the train, plane or literally even a doctor's waiting room (this last example many times over the past 12 years or so). People in that particular situation often have a lot on their minds and conversation doesn't flow too well, but I just can't seem to shut up. But because of this I have met people relevant to my life; it's almost as if they had been put there for the meet-ing to happen. I have my own thoughts on why this happens, but will keep them to myself - for now.

Anyway, once back home I had decided to read the local paper one day and an advert caught my eye.

A well-known, successful local businessman was looking to get involved in corporate entertainment, utilising what the local area of Argyll had to offer. I knew that Gordon was very close friends with my Mum's younger brother, Jim. My Uncle Jim had been a very positive influence on me growing up; he was the kind of uncle who is a great friend too, and the type I aspire to be like. So I spoke to Jim on the phone, and it was agreed that Gordon and I should talk.

While in the Marines. My SQ (Specialised Qualification) was Landing Crafts. I had followed this course after my excitement at seeing the boat troop on that day back in 1997 when I was an impressionable young fish farmer and saw the Commachio Group pass by.

While in the Corps I had also trained in a few civilian outdoor pursuits qualifications such as an RYA (Royal Yacht Association) advanced power boat instructor, a civilian summer mountain leader and rock leader and had become an RYA windsurfing instructor, so I was accumulating my certificates to enable me to become an outdoor pursuits instructor when the time came.

Anyway, I phoned Gordon and we arranged to meet for a coffee later in the week. At the meeting we had a very exciting conversation about what we could both do together. From this meeting ProAdventure Scotland was born, which was to become my first experience of business.

What I have learned over the years is you never stop learning - never - regardless of whether it's in business or just living a life.

Well, that's how it has certainly been for me. Though I would hate to think that I have become unemotional over the years, I think it's true to say that I have, up to a point. I'm sure past girlfriends would certainly agree with this. Sorry girls. It's just that I've learned through my life experiences how to protect myself, and how I do that is to never let myself be shocked. It's a bit of a negative view but I always consider the unexpected. Little did I know what 'unexpected' was going to mean for me.

42

Chapter 6 – It's Beginning To Go A Bit Pear Shaped (2004)

I was living my usual active and exciting life when things started to change with me. I had always been very sharp with my reactions. I had 20/20 vision and a never-ending supply of energy and motivation. Looking back, my life was ridiculously active, but at the time it was just my life, this was the way it had always been for me - never a dull moment. And if it was starting to look as if the pace was slowing down, I soon changed that with some snowboarding in Chamonix or windsurfing in Barbados. I had no limits when it came to living or stepping up to adventure.

I now had this fabulous opportunity to manage ProAdventure Scotland. This was a new, up-to-the-minute outdoor facility for young people, based in Dunoon. It was a fresh, bold and exciting company for the area.

My day was filled with taking powerboat courses on the River Clyde, leading mountain biking trails in the local hills, adventure walks with groups during the school holidays, or giving windsurfing lessons in the evening. You get the idea. The local area around Dunoon is ideal for introducing youngsters to these activities.

I was under a bit of 'new to me' pressure with this. I was a manager now. This was a very different work ethic to what I had been used to. When I wasn't out on the hill with one sport or another, I was in the office trying to get my head around the managerial side of business.

This involved me sitting at a desk; something that was novel to me and required a different type motivation and focus. Sitting and working at the same time was an adjustment that this former Royal Marine was making. I had always been a practical individual, where risk assessments came instantly to me while on my feet. I was good at hands-on tackling a problem on the move, and I had never had to think about them from a seat at a desk and then write them up. I could see the danger on a cliff face when looking at it before I climbed it. Now I was being asked to write up problem solutions in an office before actually getting to the cliff. This was, without a doubt, foreign to me. But I had great support from the other company staff to show me the way, correct my spelling in emails and other documents, and to teach me how to manage the practical and desk issues together. Going between the office and windsurfing lessons gave me access to two very different work ethics under the one title.

One of the many perks to this new dream job of managing Proadventure Scotland was getting the coolest company car that I could have dreamed of. A brand new silver Mitsubishi L200 Warrior. For a windsurfing-obsessed 25-year-old who had recently left the Royal Marines, this was the perfect car for my life style. As far as I was concerned life couldn't get much better! I was on this train track of awesomeness at the next juncture in my life. The way I was seeing it, everything behind me had been amazing, and now it appeared that everything in front of me would be too. I was at this next stage, now managing ProAdventure Scotland and although everything behind me had been amazing, it appeared everything in front of me would continue in this vein…

It was approaching New Year's Eve 2004 and it was arranged that a group of mates and I would bring in the bells at The Pier Hotel. This is a venue that was often used for Hogmanay by us all. It is situated in the small village of Strone, and to get there I had to drive around three miles out of Dunoon and take a slight detour via Deer Park, where a few of my friend were staying. I had agreed to pick them up en-route to the hotel. To get to Deer Park the road tracks alongside the locally-renowned river Eachaig. This was a river I had taken my brand new L200 into for a drive only the day before! This had reinforced my belief that there were no limits to the car's capabilities, and I knew that driving in and out of the river and up the steep bank was a mere walk in the park for this awesome car.

I wanted to start the New Year with a bit of excitement, and I had a plan unfolding in my head. Whilst driving though, it had failed to sink into my head that the rain was absolutely pouring down; it was torrential, bouncing off the road, and had been doing so for the majority of the evening. I should really have changed my crazy plan for this reason alone. The plan was to drive to the Pier Hotel and park up till the following day when I would pick it up.

So, I had just been to Liam's and picked up a few of my friends from Deer Park and we were now on our way to The Pier Hotel for a great night of New Year's Eve shenanigans. I thought I would start it right here and so, without warning and at a spot between the river and road where I thought I could, I threw my company car L200 Warrior off the road, down a steep bank and straight into the river! However, this same river that had been one one foot deep the day before, was now in full spate, five feet deeper and flowing aggressively.

I slammed on the brakes, but by the time the car had skidded to a kind of stop, the front end was fully submerged. The river had now taken over and the car's engine was literally being drowned at the same time it was being dragged deeper into the fast flowing River Eachaig.

I was in complete shock; I knew that at times like this you have to remain calm, and that's what I tried to do, but the reality was total inward panic at a level I had never experienced before. While writing this I have momentarily tried to put myself back into that place but I must say, I really don't like it - to the point that I'm typing faster to try and get this part finished and move on from it. I phoned a couple of my friends involved so I could hear it from their side 10 years on and it has made me feel very uncomfortable and embarrassed all over again.

We made our way out the back doors of the car, as they weren't yet in the water and so were the obvious and safest way to go. I think it's safe to say that a calm panic is what happened. Liam ran along and got his friend who had a tractor, and he came with some towing equipment and with difficultly pulled the L200 out the river and back to Deer Park where it could sit for the night.

I stood there watching this going on feeling numb along with many other emotions, none of which were positive. I have since found out the car behind, had also nearly followed me down the bank thinking it was still the road I was on.

The following day I called my good friend Richie, who's a mechanic, and see what needed to be done to get it going again – if, in fact, it could be got going again.

Why I feel the need to tell you this particular story, one of my many mad/insane stories from my life of madness and showing off, is this. That evening, I believe that the stress, embarrass-ment, humiliation and disappointment which I felt in myself released something destructive that had been living in me in the shadows my whole life.

The best way I can describe what was going on, is that It felt as if my world was a mirror that had just been smashed to pieces. I could see it all but none of it made any clear sense. It has never really got back to the way it was before and I have to say that when life goes pear shaped from time to time, which it inevitably does, this happens over again. But with time, tenacity and arrogance I did get back to putting the pieces back together; enough of the broken mirror to being able to see a way forward through life.

One particular day sticks in the memory. I was in the habit of making a coffee in the morning to start the office side of my day. I always came in, and sat at the desk with my coffee with two sugars. This day began like the others and I sat down with my coffee to look through what was on the agenda for today's activities. As I sipped my coffee I began to feel strange tingles in the tips of my toes. Sure that it was just the usual pins and needles you get when you sit awkwardly, I moved my sitting position to allow my circulation to come back. This didn't seem to sort it. Regardless of what I was doing, I could not get the circulation back into my feet. I tried standing and touching my toes, running on the spot, I even remember putting them in a bowl of warm water in case it was a chill. No change, still there.

These tingles lasted for a few weeks and my attempts to get rid of them became more exotic and imaginative - standing on my head for example. In fact it slowly progressed until it was dominating my toes, all of them. It was annoyingly hilarious, but also not right and I finally realised that this needed to be looked at by someone more qualified than this standing-on-his-head Bootneck.

Chapter 7 – Annoying

Eventually I found the telephone number. I booked myself into my local doctors' surgery.

My new doctor was not a face I recognised from around the town. He was a nice, gentle man, who naturally commanded your attention when he spoke. That was something I was used to from the Marines when I was being addressed by a superior rank.

I went through the usual check-up stuff, answering questions, being prodded about, having my blood pressure taken and so on. So far, so standard. And then he gave me the awful diagnosis.

"You have trapped a nerve in your spine." This was what was causing these annoying tingles and I was told that I needed anti-inflammatory medication to calm it down. It had to be dealt with fast to stop it progressing.

I am proud to admit that, until that point, I was so fit and healthy I hadn't even known my doctor's name.

I took the anti-inflammatories for a couple of weeks, but I was confused; they weren't making a jot of difference to this bloody trapped nerve. In fact, I was sure it was spreading still further into my feet.

After the two weeks there was no other option but to visit the doctor again. I went along, slightly embarrassed about returning in the space of two weeks. Oh man, it was the same lady behind the counter booking me in. She must have thought I was a right hypochondriac.

In I went and told the GP the tingles were still there. In fact they were more intense. They had actually spread, despite taking the tablets. I have to admit I was slightly annoyed at being given the wrong anti-inflammatories and having to go back for another visit. I was not used to wasting my time - well that was how I saw it then.

The GP carried out some more tests in his thorough and thoughtful way, and asked more questions. What happened next was not expected. He advised me that it would be quickest, and best, to send me across the Clyde for a more thorough check. He explained that the back is a complex area of the body and any number of problems could be the reason.

"I'll book you in for an MRI scan. That will tell us exactly what is going on." Surely this was overkill? Until now I had thought MRIs were only for the very ill. But for checking a basic trapped nerve? Hmmm.

It's not like the tingles were anything more than annoying. And 'annoying' was something I had total control over. I had learned in the Marines how to deal with annoying. How to carry on your life completely normally with 'annoying' sitting on your shoulder.

Blisters on your feet during a 30-mile booted run across Dartmoor were annoying, but not a show stopper. I remember one lad had just finished such a run or a march. One of his toe nails had come off towards the end of the run. It made its way down his sock to his heel and then started to cut into his foot, like an old fashioned tin opener. He had a flappy heel by the end of the day. It was annoying, but his focus wasn't too affected. His focus was the finish. Once you have lived with annoying for a while, it just becomes background noise, I promise.

Another example of annoying was when one of the six in your room was a snorer. He would keep the other five awake to the point that in the morning his bed would be surrounded by boots or whatever other non-lethal hard object you could throw.

Annoying was more and more manageable as time passed. If you choose to focus on annoying, then you are in big trouble. Annoying will grow if you let it. It will eat at you given the chance, snap you like a twig. Ask yourself: "Are you a twig?" Keep annoying under control and you are still the boss, regardless of what's going on. Get this under your control then you can ramp up your level of tolerating annoying to pretty much any point that's required.

Chapter 8 – A Backless Gown And A Fabulous Day Out

The closest MRI machine was at the Royal Alexandra Hospital in Paisley near Glasgow. No big deal. To get there I had to take a 30-minute ferry crossing the Clyde from Dunoon on the Cowal Peninsula over to Gourock, and then it was a 30-minute drive up the M8 motorway.

I didn't know it at the time, but this would turn out to be the first of three required tests that I must fail in order to be told what I had already worked out for myself. I know what I've got. It's a trapped nerve. Why don't they just find it? Now!

I had heard of 'MRI', but it was only later that I found out it means Magnetic Resonance Imaging and it makes very detailed images of soft things, like organs. I have heard it can look at bones and teeth too. It is very good at finding brain tumours. For anyone undergoing it, the best thing is that there's no radiation involved. It all sounds like wizard stuff to me now. I was told how lucky I was to be getting into this thing.

Lucky comes in all shapes I guess. At the time I didn't feel too lucky.

So, I was experiencing annoying tingles in my toes. I was delighted these tingles were about to be fixed. All my ducks were in a row now and I headed to Glasgow in the car.

I wasn't familiar with hospitals. They weren't for me. Hospitals, in my mind, were for ill people. Yet here I was, walking through hospital corridors looking for the scanning department. All new to me but something I had to do. Really, it was not a problem. In fact I was there for them to deal with a problem. This alone was novel - me with a health problem! That's a laugh. I must be getting old.

To add to my discomfort hospitals have this smell that goes hand in hand with them. A smell of things being cleaned; it's like TCP or something. Sensations like noticing the smell and the strange noises made me feel sad for the poor souls that were in the hospital. From time to time I would see a very ill person, and that put me on edge.

When I was being brought up my parents had told me not to stare at people in wheelchairs; that it was rude. Being in the hospital was making this built-in standard hard to adhere to, as ill people seemed to be everywhere, even more so in the department where I was heading.

As I walked into the MRI section I met a girl who was at school with my big sister Nicola. We recognised one another immediately and exchanged smiles; she would have remembered me being a cheeky younger brother of her friend some ten years before. It turned out she was controlling the machine for my check-up. How bizarre, but a typical Dunoon coincidence. Over the years I have met people from Dunoon randomly all over the world - that's small towns for you.

This was a busy place. There was practically a conveyor belt of ill people coming in to use this department and its machines. Fortunately, I was the healthiest person there. Some of the poor souls there would have brought a tear to your eye.

I was given a brief on what was about to happen. Lynn and I had a quick laugh with a five-minute catch up while she started preparing me. The only way I could describe the place was that it was like something out of a James Bond movie with all the nurses who operated the machine behind a thick glass screen in another room. I was actually enjoying this experience. You can't be stressed about a trapped nerve. Being in the Marines got me to some very sensitive places and I saw some super cool stuff. This was much the same. I was getting to have this very small yet scary insight to the world of a seriously ill person while being a healthy guy - lucky me!

Lynn took great pleasure in handing me the white gown I was to wear; you know, the ones that don't fasten up the back. She had a cheeky kind of 'you'll like this' smile on her face as she passed it over. I had to go into the small room at the side of the machine and put it on. It's funny how a man's pride works. A white gown that doesn't tie up at the back? Not keen on this bit.

I was led to the sliding bed for the machine and shown where to lie down. I was then swept over with a handheld metal detector, to make sure I didn't have any metal in my body that I had forgotten to mention. Then I was briefed on the rubber safety panic button, which was a handheld pump ball. Would I panic? You know the answer to that one! Finally, I was fitted with padding under my legs and at the sides of my head to keep me in position for the scan. It had to be accurate. This meant me not moving.

During the MRI machine briefing beforehand, I was advised that it was very noisy and they would give me headphones and music while I was inside the scanner. The machine was huge, yet inside it was cramped, noisy, and very warm, but for the length of time you are in it didn't matter how uncomfortable it was. Its purpose is what's paramount, so everything else takes a back seat.

I have never been one to get claustrophobic, but I have to admit it was a tight one in there. The rubber hand pump was your panic button. Squeeze that and it informed the medical team that you wanted out, and in a hurry! I wondered how many stressed-out worried sweaty hands had held it before me.

The scan lasted around 45 minutes. It was super exciting, as noisy as a rock concert and the noise seemed to be alive. It moved around the machine. Every so often a voice would come over my headphones explaining the situation and what was coming next. They were always very courteous and asked me if everything was ok. That was a simple one to answer. I was getting all this exciting attention in a billion pound machine with a load of nurses running around me at my beck and call. And I wasn't even ill! What a fabulous day out I was having. But I did feel bit of a fraud at the same. To add to this exciting day, the tingles in my toes would soon be taken care of, forever.

Finally, the machine stopped and I was pulled out on the table by a different woman. I was slightly disappointed. I wanted some more of the old school banter with Lynn. This other woman was gentle, quieter, and the type of woman who walks around you on eggshells.

She said they had looked at the scan and all seemed fine, as far as they could tell. My Initial thought was a confused 'great'. They have not found anything - that's good! I was a bit surprised, confused, and pleased. Then she carried on: "To save time and avoid you having to come back up here from Dunoon, we're going to scan your head."

Yeah cool, I was impressed with how efficient and thorough they were. It was obvious I was being given the VIP treatment. After all it was Lynn who was operating the machine, so they were just being meticulous. I was also slightly disappointed. I was hungry. I had already planned my McDonald's stop on the way back to the ferry and home.

This time though, I had a very serious head brace put on me, along with a number of seeds being planted in my mind. The brace was to make certain that your head didn't move in the scanner and spoil the pictures. There was a tiny mirror in front of the brace. It let you see the controllers and was intended to make you feel less isolated. Well, that was the idea anyway.

It was Friday afternoon. I thought they would want to finish for the weekend, but they know what they're doing. They were saving my time; they didn't want a repeat journey from me up for another test. It suited me too. I was getting bored with this scene and to tell you the truth, I wouldn't have been too impressed to be called back to have my head examined, just for my sore feet!

Off I went, back into the machine.

At the time, I didn't know much about my body other than by Marine standards. I could do 20 of the hardest forward-facing pull ups, 117 press ups, and run a 5 minutes and 15 seconds mile. This scan made me think "what are they playing at? I have pins and needles in my toes, not my bloody head."

I was pulled out of the machine by the same woman again, not Lynn. She was still there, but in the other room, through the screens, and at the furthest away point too. I wanted to say thank you to her, and let her know I would tell Nicola that we met. I tried to catch her attention, but she kept her head down, busy at her work, and no doubt too busy to look up and give me a smile and a wave.

Chapter 9 – Everlong

I left Lynn to her work and made my way to the car to start my journey back to Dunoon.

I have always had a brilliant sense of direction. I never get lost. Whether on a mountain or in a city, my built-in compass was strong. Getting out of the hospital though was confusing, with a couple of wrong turns along the way. This wasn't like me, particularly when I had just walked this route only a couple of hours before.

At the time, I was driving my Mitsubishi 4x4 L200 company car. It was ideal for the work I was involved in and where I lived. Its height also helped because it sat higher than the others in the car park and this made it easy to find, particularly when my mind was seemingly elsewhere.

I remember that as I had arrived at the hospital before the scan I had been listening to the Foo Fighters CD on the stereo. Just as I pulled into the hospital it had arrived at my favourite song 'Everlong'. In true CD fashion, Everlong had somehow been scratched, probably due to my usual delicate and careful handling of my CDs - remove from the CD player and throw like a Frisbee into the back seat. I switched the car off just as it was starting to jump repeatedly: "Everlong, I've waited here for you … Everlong, I've waited here for you … Everlong, I've …"

I was back in the car and heading home. It's hard to describe what was happening to me then. Everything seemed to be on auto pilot, upside down, surreal. Yes I was driving, and safely. In fact I was driving in the slow lane, which wasn't like me at all. I do not drive in the slow lane.

I was also deep in thought. Two questions kept coming back. Why did they do the extra scan? Had Lynn been avoiding me? In this strange mental state, I found myself at the ferry terminal – with no memory of actually getting there.

When I had been in the MRI machine, I had spent a good part of the time thinking about McDonald's because I was really hungry. But now I was not. Good job really, as I don't even remember driving past McDonald's.

I pulled into the ferry car park and was grateful that a ferry was alongside already and I was able to drive straight on. It was only once on the ferry, and parked, that I realised my Foo Fighters CD was still jumping with 'Everlong, I've waited here for you' going over and over and over. Had I been listening to that the whole way down the road and not noticed?

This was not me! I was always very aware of my surroundings regardless of what was going on; I was always in control of my thoughts, to the point that my focus from time to time pissed friends off.

Why the second scan? Was Lynn avoiding me after it? How will I tell my parents how the day went? Maybe the day did go fine, and I'm over-analysing things in my usual fashion. Are these tingles in my toes getting worse?

Why all these questions about a trapped nerve?

A trapped nerve???

I am a class act when it comes to living the statement 'no cuff too tough', so a weekend of winging it with the questions from my parents and colleagues about my MRI scan was about to kick off.

But unfortunately, so too was my imagination. On the face of it, I would just carry on with life as if nothing was amiss to avoid further detailed questions and conversations I didn't want to have. The fact was, I didn't know anything other than what my own imagination had decided.

The weekend was almost over. What was becoming more apparent to me was it made no difference whether tomorrow was a Monday or a Sunday. What day it was had no relevance. I needed answers now. The chaos that was going on in my head was overpowering.

Why the second scan? And why was it so quick? Why did the second nurse tell me the first scan was fine, but yet they didn't mention the outcome of the second? If the second one had been fine too, surely she would have said. If it wasn't though, she wouldn't have said, surely that's for a doctor to say! I was feeling sick, physically sick.

Chapter 10 – Reaching Out

I knew where a few doctors lived in Dunoon. Would it be overstepping the mark to go and knock on their doors at ten o'clock on a Sunday night? I needed answers though. I needed someone to tell me that what was going on in my head was not just in my head, or even better that it was just in my head! I was totally out of control; pacing the house from room to room.

An old school friend had a mum who was a local doctor. I used to visit the house a lot and she had known me since primary school. I thought she would be a good person to approach at this unsociable time, on a Sunday evening. They lived out of town. I got in the car and started the drive there. By this point, if my car had broken down, then I would have either run for it or stolen a car. I decided I was going. That was it. I was determined to see her and that decision was already beginning to relax me. She was a doctor and I would listen to her more than I was listening to myself.

I finally got to her house. I pulled into her garden and there was no car in the drive. No-one was home. This exacerbated my inner panic. I had taken the step to overstep the mark and it had fallen flat. What now?

I drove down the drive to turn. The only way to manoeuvre this large car was at the bottom of the drive, next to the house. When I was turning I stopped the car. I broke down and cried like a child. I cried out a weekend of unknown stress. It was ten o'clock on a Sunday night and I had nowhere to turn. I was alone and, to be honest, that's where I wanted to be. I wanted to be alone. I didn't want to upset the people close to me, the ones that when I'd had a problem before had unconditionally helped me. I was panicking and I didn't quite know why. This billion pound machine on Friday, what the fuck had it found? No trapped nerve in this body. Just tingling toes!

I was now lying against the steering wheel of the car, sobbing for what must have been a good ten minutes. I finally pulled myself back to an acceptable level of normality. I started to do the usual preparing to drive routine, start the car, seatbelt, mirror checks, and then, suddenly, I saw her car pulling into the drive. 10.30 On a Sunday night. She had been away for the weekend and this was them just getting back. My state of mind had been strangely changed, and I was now feeling that I had been caught somewhere I shouldn't really be. It's amazing how a cry can readjust your thinking.

"Paul, is everything ok?" It was obvious I had just been crying and the last time she had seen me crying was when I was nine and I had skinned my knee when out playing with Robin, her son, strangely enough in this very garden. Here I was crying in their garden again, only some 20 years on.

I was invited in and offered a coffee. I sat in silence. It was tough trying to find the correct way to put my worries across.

I had nothing more than a hunch to go on and I felt I needed something more tangible than a hunch to justify this Sunday night visit.

I explained what had happened on Friday and why I had just had the weekend from hell. I apologised for my visit and I told her that I knew that it was intrusive. She made me feel much better and said that she knew my GP well. She said she would phone him in the morning and let him know what I had told her. I left their house feeling much better about things, and so incredibly grateful to her for taking the time to listen to me.

Chapter 11 - They Don't Deserve This

The next day at work was just a normal Monday. I had a full day booked in - mountain biking, windsurfing, and power boating all in the same day, and with the same crowd. In that situation you get to know the group well and them you.

Getting to sleep that weekend had been tough, although after I had spoken with my friend's mum I felt a lot better. The combination of the sleepless nights and the relief of having spoken to the doctor meant that on the Sunday night I went out like a light.

Waking up with worry though was something that I wasn't used to. I didn't realise it until now, but my life had been so uncomplicated until that weekend. My idea of worry until this point had been along the lines of 'Was buying that new mountain bike irresponsible?' Or, 'Do I have enough money to go out this weekend?' Probably not, but I'm going out anyway!

This new constant nagging worry was keeping my mind off my daily job. I was meant to take a group of youngsters out mountain biking and windsurfing. I had to cancel. It would have been irresponsible to go ahead with the day's activities the way I was feeling.

My focus was on seeing that GP. Did I want to? I had to. He might have good news for me. He might not! He might have no news for me. The day dragged on, and so did my concern. It was all I could think of. Would my GP have information – but what kind? Would I want to hear it? Possibly, possibly not.

Round and round my head went these questions. Whatever he had to tell me, I had to hear it, no matter how dire it was, I had to know.

I didn't book an appointment, I just went. Formalities had gone out the window now. The place was packed for afternoon surgery, and with people who had booked appointments. I told the receptionist that I had to see my GP. She looked up and said straight faced: "Sorry, your doctor is fully booked today. If you would like to make an appointment, he is free at 5.15pm on Thursday."

Mentally holding it together that afternoon, standing in the middle of the busy, doctors' surgery was one of the hardest things I have ever done. As I was starting to explain it was very important that I see my doctor now, I was given a miracle. He came out to the front desk to give the woman some mail to post. He took one look at me across the desk, pointed at me and said: "My office. Now, Paul."

I don't know if you have ever experienced your body doing what it knows it has to do, but your mind really doesn't want to do it. Even if my mind had said 'stop', my body would have kept going. Until this point, it had always been the other way for me. My body would say 'please can I stop?' and my mind had always said, 'just a bit further'. I didn't realise it at the time, but this was about to become a familiar, regular feeling for me.

I followed the doctor into his surgery. He sat me down across the desk from him. And he said in his usual calming way: "I've spoken with Royal Alexandra today Paul. They have found complications with your brain."

Er, what? What - ? What complications? Are these why I have numb feet? This was making no sense.

He went on: "Reading between the lines, I would say you have lesions on your brain."

What does this mean? How was I going to tell my parents?

He said he would come to my parents' house at 7 o'clock that evening, once surgery was finished, and talk to us all about it. By that time, he would have more definite answers from the Royal Alexandra to discuss with us.

I left the surgery in a daze. I walked across the stony path outside, and leaned against the wall. I slid down and put my broken head in my hands. I tried to make sense of what I had just been told. I would love to know what happened next. But I don't. What really happened in the hour that followed? I have absolutely no idea.

The next memory I have of this day was getting to my parents' house. I knew I had to tell them what had happened, but I didn't know how I was going to do it. I had a thousand questions myself, about something I knew nothing about, so how was I going to answer their own inevitable questions?

Mum and Dad had known about my numb toes, and that I had been for an MRI to find where the trapped nerve was, but that was it. My anxiety after my MRI I had kept to myself. I didn't visit them that weekend and I hadn't said anything about Nicola's friend, or about my head scan. All they had known from a phone call was that 'it went well'.

Dad was already home from work but Mum wasn't back yet. He was in the kitchen when I went in.

"I've got something to tell you." Dad knew me very well. He knew exactly how I approached him when I was about to tell him bad news. In the past it had been stuff like: "Em, Dad I was caught smoking at school today", or "Dad I crashed your car into a taxi today!" How trivial these old items of 'bad' news now seemed to me.

"It's about my MRI scan and it's important." Dad is a very level-headed man. He calls a spade a spade and when it comes to panic situations he is calm and collected. He is ex-Glasgow police and not much fazes him. He sat in silence while he adjusted to the news and then said: "'Well, if I'm not mistaken, that could be any number of things, many of which aren't serious."

While we were in the kitchen, and I had just dropped this bombshell, Mum pulled up in the car. Dad went out to see her. I made my way out just after him. He was giving her a cuddle and telling her: "He's had some bad news, but everything will be fine, just listen to me. Listen to Paul, but stay calm."

While Dad was telling Mum this, she was already getting worked up asking what it was. "What is it Paul?"

I walked up to mum in the back garden. I realised I had started crying.

It wasn't fair what I was going to say. My parents didn't deserve this. They are good people and amazing parents. What right did I have to come to the house that day and drop this on them? They have only ever loved me, and been there for me, and here I was putting this on them.

I told her that after the MRI on Friday they had found some complications with my brain and that I possibly had lesions on it.

"What does this mean? Paul what does that mean? Vic, what does this mean?"

76

Chapter 12 – You're No Windsurfing Instructor, Man

I had been instructing at ProAdventure Scotland for six months when I started to get the tingles in my toes. I now knew that they were down to the lesions on my brain.

The doctors had been doing further tests trying to find out what was going on. I was going along with it, but only up to a point. I had agreed to pretty much everything - bar a lumbar puncture. I would not let them do the lumbar puncture. I had done the eye tests, blood tests, MRI scans, and reaction tests but I wouldn't let them do a lumbar puncture - the final test. And this was to be the one that would decide what was wrong.

While this was going on, so was ProAdventure Scotland. It was requiring more focus from me and therefore giving me more stress. Unfortunately these were not things I could afford to give.

Since my initial anxiety about my condition I had managed to get myself back down to earth but this was taking up a lot of my energy. I had numb feet and lesions on my brain but nothing else. I was aware that stress of the office kind is not good for me, you know, the type that keeps you up through the night. Stress of the physical kind was where I had always excelled.

I could no longer give ProAdventure what it required, and certainly what it deserved. I thought long and hard about it and finally made my decision. I went to the Managing Director and resigned. It was not easy, but the situation was such that I had to stop. Had I stayed, it would have been unfair to us all. But it did mean I could be facing unemployment and financial uncertainty.

A month after I left ProAdventure I started at Quadmania Scotland. I was the quad bike and shooting instructor.

During the month between jobs I chose to escape the challenging time I was having. I decided to visit Stevie and Paula, my friends in Barbados. Stevie had moved out there some ten years before as a chartered accountant. He had settled into life with Paula, a local girl. I had previously completely milked the benefit of having friends living in this gorgeous place. This was to be another one of those times.

I had been out the year before with my friend Mitch on a windsurfing and drinking week. The windsurfing in Barbados is out this world - and the drinking is a close second. This was a very different holiday from that one. No drinking whatsoever. I planned to relax, eat Paula's good food, and sit on the beach, and sunbathe. Admittedly, this was not the usual me, but something told me that it was time to take it easy.

Stevie and I did a couple of late evening runs when he got home from work. Nothing too excessive, I think we did maybe a 10-miler and the rest were just the kind of five-milers that I was used to running regularly. But they were tougher than usual. Stevie is a great runner and until then we had been well-matched. But these runs were tougher. Surely it was just the change in temperature, and the humidity? The weather was dragging these five miles out to seem like 20.

I was down on the beach sunning one day and I thought, stuff it. I'll go windsurfing. When I left Scotland, I had no desire at all to windsurf. I purposely didn't take my kit with me and had to hire some. It's strange the times that stick in your head when you let them. At home, if I had I been out windsurfing, cars would pull over at the side of the road to watch me. I was at a level that I was proud of reaching. A lot of my friends, Mitch included, were far better than me. I could hold my own though, regardless of the sea state or the wind strength.

Down I went to the Silver Sands surf shack and said that I'd like to hire some kit. When the young man asked what stage I was at, I requested certain kit. He knew right away that I must know what I was doing. Even the way you word it makes a difference.

Before going out, I had the usual banter with this lad in the shack. I told him I was a windsurfing instructor, just so he'd be happy with me going out on the advanced kit and in the current wind. The wind was ideal for me. Cross-on-shore and of strength that would give me some fast fun. I carried the kit to the waterline on my head - at the time this was how the good guys did it!

I put the board in the water and just jumped onto it from the shore. The second I was on it I went ripping off - and then wiped out. How embarrassing. It was OK though, I was a wee bit off the shore, and with lots of wind, so I just went for the slightly advanced water start. This is when you use the sail and the wind to pull you up out of the water and straight into planning, a fast cool manoeuvre. I flew the sail in the wind, got it all in place, and it pulled me out of the water and immediately threw me right over the other side - back into the water.

I didn't understand this. How and why is this happening? I had the perfect kit. The wind was ideal for me. And yet it felt and looked as if I had no idea about what I was doing. What was going on?

Anyway, after half an hour of getting a kicking between the beach and the water, and spending the majority of the time on the shoreline, embarrassed and very confused I carried the kit back up to the surf shack. I even carried it in the easier, less advanced way of the board and sail down by my side.

I handed it all back to the surf shack. And I will never forget what the guy said, the same bloke I had been having the banter with. He looked at me as if I was a liar and said: "You're no windsurfing instructor man".

I couldn't even argue with him, despite the fact I had been

managing a centre and instructing windsurfing just two weeks before. What was happening to me? This experience put me into a severely despondent mood that I couldn't seem to shake.

However, I carried on with my final few days on Barbados having tough runs with Stevie in the evenings, followed by Paula's great cooking, but with no windsurfing during the day. For some reason, the sport that I labelled myself as splendid at, was for the time being, out of my reach.

Chapter 13 – I Go On A Date

I came back to Scotland and had a couple of weeks of downtime before I was due to start at Quadmania. I was looking forward to this new job. It was completely different, but still in the same vein as the work I'd been doing at ProAdventure.

I was out with some friends on the Saturday night before I started at Quadmania. It was the usual Saturday pub night in Dunoon. To be honest, I wasn't really drinking, and it just didn't appeal to me. I had a bit too much going on in my life. Returning from the Barbados stint, I was really low on cash. I was about to start a new job. To top it off I had two numb feet.

Anyway, we all ended up back at a local girl's house. Annette ran a very popular hair dressing salon in the town, and she was well known for throwing good parties. She also employed Sarah, a particularly stunning girl. Sarah had knocked me back for a night out a fair few times over the years of being a Marine. The more she did that, the greater my interest in her became. She was quiet; the type of girl who didn't say more than she needed. Other than giving me unnecessary haircuts over the years we had never really talked. But she was at this party and, as fate would have it, we got talking. It turned out that we got on well. She agreed to go out with me for a drink one night that week. That lifted my morale, I can tell you.

On our night out it became apparent very quickly that we were relaxed in one another's company and there was a real air of trust between us. We were both invited to Annette's house that Friday for dinner, and I think it must have been apparent to both Annette and her husband Mark that we were both happy with what was unfolding.

When helping clear the table Annette quietly had a wee word in my ear. I will always remember it because it proved to be true and, in time, was tested to the highest level. What she said was: "Paul I have never met anyone more committed than Sarah. When it comes to honesty, she says it as it is." All of this proved to be true over the next four years we spent together.

And what's more, it was about to be very severely tested.

Chapter 14 – Quad Bikes And Collie Dogs (2005)

In my new job I was going to be teaching people how to shoot, and how to ride quad bikes into the hills. There was not the added stress of the managerial side of the business. I could get into this new job and, quite honestly, the job and the Quad-mania team played a key supportive part in what was to come.

The job was great in every way and perfect for me at this time in my life. I was getting out on the hills, either on the quad bikes or taking groups out for clay-pigeon target shooting. And then at the end of the day I could go home, forget about work, and then get up eager to start again the following day. Bliss.

The beauty of the quad biking was that my numb feet didn't really matter. It's not as if I was walking all day. The worst thing that happened was that being on the bikes often gave me a numb bum. So the feet just added to the numb theme.

Quadmania is on Stronchullin, a working farm. The owner David was mainly on farm-based work, and I took the quad biking. I would see him from time to time through the day. He would come walking off the hill with one of his loyal working dogs at his side. Usually he had 'Dusk' or, as he was suitably nicknamed, 'Smelly'. Smelly had taught me a valuable lesson which would stick with me. Never pat a working farm dog. Patting him told me how he'd got the nickname.

I liked the look of that farm dog's unconditional love for his owner. I began to think. I could take a dog to work with me, and it could either hang out at the farm or come out and run beside me on the quad treks. Collies can also ride on your quad bike quite happily when needed. Super cool!

I was now living full-time with Sarah. I don't actually remember a day that I moved in with her. It just happened over time. After some persuasion, Sarah agreed to go along with the idea of us having a dog, but she made it clear it was my responsibility. I bought the yellow paper and searched the ads for my new friend.

I found a farm in Mauchline, near Ayr on the west coast that was selling Collie puppies. We decided to drive down the following Sunday and 'just have a wee look'. If anything, it was a nice drive and it would give us a good idea whether we should eventually go ahead with having a dog. Maybe once Twinkle, the cat, passed away … or something.

The car journey home with Kyle, our new puppy, was a fun one. Twinkle was going to love getting to know him.

Kyle was easy to look after at work. Quadmania is well-equipped for taking care of a wee Collie pup. No harm could come to him, and by home time he was tired from a good day on the farm, chasing and being chased by the other dogs. All in all, Kyle was a good plan - for the present anyway.

Things were nice and straightforward. I had a fun nine to five job that fitted my lifestyle. I drove a company Land Rover on wet days and my own Wrangler Jeep on sunny days. Kyle was always at my side. I had even bought a farmer's flat cap to wear when walking him. Things were simple, rewarding, and stress free. What more could I have wanted? The numbness in my right toes was still there, but I didn't pay too much attention to that. The toes were just a bit less than an annoying background noise, the kind of thing you tune out to after a while.

I came in to the farm kitchen one day for lunch and David asked: "Have you gone over on your ankle or something Paul? You've got quite a bad limp there. You know, if you were a horse I reckon I'd just shoot you."

I had noticed it, but I had chosen to ignore it. I knew I had a limp. I also knew it was because my numb toes had this morning spread up into my right foot. Very weirdly and obviously completely unrelated I also noticed that my eyes were behaving strangely. It was very subtle but when you have 20/20 vision, even a slight change is easy to notice. Things right in front of me were fine to see. Things at the side had become harder to find.

The background noise had just got noisier. To add to that, I had been told that morning by Sarah and now by David to go and talk to my GP. I had to bite the bullet again and go and discuss everything that I was noticing.

I had been having a good run of things with my job. I was resigned to the fact that these numb toes would just go away at some point, on their own, with no doctors. Looking back as I'm writing this, I was really just lying to myself the whole time. I had a problem. I was concerned it was going to come along some day and bite me on the bum.

I had not seen my GP or discussed things with him for around six months, so a good consultation with him was obviously in order. What harm could it do? Maybe things had changed, and due to this he'd know what was wrong with me. He'd possibly even be able to give me medication to sort it.

Chapter 15 – Lying To Myself And Everyone Else

I sat with my GP and brought him up to date with the past eight months of numb feet, but nothing else, and then the past few days of a limp and strange vision. He asked me again to go for a lumbar puncture. And again, I refused. He was fine with that, as he was starting to get to know me a wee bit.

Looking at my history and the type of person I was, he would have gathered I was the stubborn sort. Once I had my mind set on doing something, or in this case not doing something, then that was that.

The next couple of weeks were tough and getting tougher rather faster than I wanted. These weeks involved a lot of lying to Paul. As I was lying to myself, I was passing duff information to everyone else too. It was not a case of me knowingly lying to them, but more a case of telling them the same as I was telling myself. It made it more believable to me when I said it aloud. But I'm sure they could see what I seemed to choose to ignore.

One Sunday, I came out of the house and made my way to the car. I got in and started the eight-mile drive in the Land Rover. Then quite suddenly I was sure I was blind. I was just coming out of Sandbank, about two miles from home. What on earth had happened? I was not blind in the way you would normally consider it. I still had vision. But it made no sense. I had no idea how close or far away things were. My best way of describing it is I was seeing the world as if through a kaleidoscope.

I pulled over to the side of the road. With very great difficultly I phoned my parents' home. The difficulty was both physical and mental. I asked Mum to relax but then I said: "I am on the Sandbank High Road and I can't see right."

Strangely, I had pulled over outside the cemetery where my grandparents whom I loved so much are buried. "And Mum, can someone come for me please? Actually, I can't see."

Chapter 16 – All Tapped Out

Sitting there at the side of the road, waiting for my mother to come and pick me up, hardly able to see the road for the tears and the weird visual effects, I made a decision there and then. I would get the lumbar puncture. I would have that final test that was holding things up. Until that day I had no real reason to want to know what was wrong with me. That day though, I did.

My limp was unworkable. And my vision was appalling. As I was finding out, while living through this, there's only so much running from life that you can do until you can't run another step to get away from your problems. That's where I was, with my back to a wall.

I phoned my GP and had an uncomfortable conversation. I brought him up to date with my new situation and I actually asked him if I could go for the lumbar puncture, and as soon as possible too. You have probably gathered that deep down I knew that I would have to have one at some point. The time had come. What's more, I reckon my GP had been expecting a phone call from me about then.

Sarah took me up to the Glasgow Southern General Hospital and she'd already offered to come in with me. She knew I was not looking forward to this test or its outcome. This was a new hospital to me, but one that I would come to know only too well.

My appointment was at the Neurological Department on the 4th floor. Again, this hospital was a devil of a place to find a place to park. But I had to be choosy these days, as my limp was awful.

Once in Neurology I didn't like what I was seeing. Very ill people, the type who until then I'd only seen in passing, and only on TV. I stopped to ask a nurse for directions outside the room of an unconscious bald girl. She had what looked like 100 electrodes attached to her head. While I was there, alarm bells started to sound and this girl, the girl lying right in front of me, started to have a fit. Doctors and nurses came running into the room and started to treat her while shouting to one another. One nurse came over and closed the blinds. I shuddered and didn't dare look at Sarah.

We carried on walking, in silence, until we came to another desk. I was checked in and Sarah and I were shown into a waiting room. We sat very still, hardly speaking. A wee bit of small talk passed between us about how it was such a modern and clean building. Apart from that we said nothing. I really didn't want to talk about what was coming. I knew that on days like these you just go with it. You speak to who you must and you do what you are told. You don't focus on them though. You just go with them. I think this approach was definitely instilled by the Marines. You may not like what's about to happen, and yes, you don't know what the outcome will be. But you have to do it. You don't have a choice. It's the old grit.

Eventually I was called for my appointment and we were shown into a room by a young woman. She introduced herself as Dr Stratton and explained that she would be doing my lumbar puncture. She was nice. Relaxed! She asked if I had any questions as she handed me the all-too-familiar open-back gown. She involved Sarah in the conversation and explained what Sarah could do to help me. We agreed that I would lie along the short bed. Sarah would sit in a seat at the end of it. She would have my head on her lap and she'd talk gently to me, keeping me relaxed as well as she could.

That's what she did.

Dr Stratton had gathered I was not looking forward to this. She felt down my spine with her fingers, going between my vertebrae. She finally stopped, with her fingers quite low on my spine.

She said: "I think we will try here Paul. How does that feel to you?"

I had to lie: "Yeah that feels fine." Physically it did, but mentally it didn't. I was controlling an inward panic. I wasn't being macho, just quiet and saying no more than answering the questions I was asked. I was not in a chatty mood.

She got a little needle out and explained that there would be a slight pinprick and that would numb me, 'just like at the dentist'. This would then make the spinal tap far easier for me.

I did recognise a change in the name of the test here; this would have normally been something that I would have been interested in learning more about. But to be honest this just exacerbated my fear. I did however remember there was a fictional rock band many years ago called Spinal Tap. I remembered I didn't find them much better than I was finding this experience.

Ten minutes passed waiting for my back to go numb and then she started. Despite being numb I felt an almighty pressure on my lower spine, but very strangely, not where she had numbed me, nor was it near where she was 'tapping'; it was about four inches lower. You know the way the dentist works on a tooth but it's not that tooth you have the feeling on? Well, similar to that.

I was delighted to hear her next remark. She said: "It's going well. Not much more and that's you!"

I was then taken through to a room with six beds. Only one was free. I was wheeled in and asked to lie still. If I had stood and walked around too quickly, apparently, an air bubble that was in my spine would make its way up to my head, get into my brain, and result in the most awful headache. I can assure you that I lay in that bed and did not move any single part of me for two hours. Sarah sat patiently at my side. My God - What must she have been thinking about this?

The next week I did improve. I fell back into my normal life as well as I could. My limp improved. But it didn't go completely. My eyesight 'relaxed'. I went back to work a couple of days after the lumbar puncture. I was nowhere near being back to myself though. David decided not to let me take the treks but instead just to help out where I could. Looking back, I would say I was anything but a help. My eyes were still 'different' and my limp was going, but it was certainly still there.

Later that week I developed a fearful, truly unbearable, excruciating pain in my back. It was right behind my shoulder blade, where I couldn't seem to get it to relax at all. I couldn't carry on at work any longer that day. I had to call my Mum to come and get - yet again.

At the time, I wasn't driving. Sarah had run me the eight miles and dropped me off at work that morning. People were really doing all they could for me. Work was letting me come in no matter how little I could do. People were running me around, doing the best they could to help keep me feeling normal.

Mum arrived at the farm and as soon as she got there, she could see that I was in a lot of pain. I manoeuvred myself into her car.

Once I was in, I broke down. Yes. I was living a lie. I saw all that was going on with me. I recognised the worry in everyone's faces and voices. I understood that people were just wrapping me up in cotton wool with their help and smiles. They, too, were trying to face our situation. I was trying to keep going. They were letting me. I realised I was tired, so tired. I could not carry on like this. Mum ran me to Sarah's and I went to bed and slept for hours and hours.

It was the mega stubborn Marine in me that I'd been riding on these past few weeks. I had experienced being physically tired before, and yes, up to this very level. But the Commando could stop for ten minutes and his energy would return and then he'd crack on again. But I just would not stop, and people would not try and stop me. They recognised stubborn too. The only way I could accept what was going on was to make decisions for myself. And the time of knowing it all was rapidly approaching. What used to be the annoying background noise had become deafening.

Chapter 17 – Another Learning Curve

Over the last week I had found it easier walking with my hill-walking sticks, the telescopic ones that I'd used before when going up a mountain. But the day after the lumbar puncture I wasn't going to even try to go to work. I simply could not walk. And to add to this, my right arm and fist had closed up. How quickly all this developed. I can hardly believe the speed of it when I look back.

Mum called by for me and we went, yet again, to the GP for another visit. Again, looking back I can laugh. I was called into his surgery over the speaker. Mum had stayed with me every step of the way and was opening doors for me and helping where she could. I slowly made my way into the GP's consulting room. My legs were going everywhere. My sticks were sliding around on the floor. The doctor kept his eyes on me while reaching over to his phone. I hadn't even sat down and he was making arrangements. He just said: "Slightly unsteady on your feet I see, Paul".

He phoned Inverclyde Royal Hospital there and then and booked me a bed. I sat on the seat in front of him. I broke down again. While crying I managed to gulp: "I'm so tired, so tired. I need help."

By the time we had crossed the water in the ferry and made our way to Inverclyde it was late in the day and I was taken straight in to the ward. They gave me a course of intravenous steroids. These were like the rest of this, completely new to me - intravenous anything, and steroids to boot. It was weird. They had a strange chemical taste in my mouth. Another learning curve for me. I was learning too much about my body through all of this. From lesions on my brain making my toes numb, to tasting the steroids that were being administered through the vein in my arm.

What next?

The body is mad.

Here I was in hospital, unable to control my left leg and arm, and I was being pumped intravenously full of steroids. This was only two weeks after the lumbar puncture.

They told me that a neurologist would be visiting me in the morning; a doctor I already knew from the consultation some six months ago. He too had wanted me to get a lumbar puncture back then. He could not make a full diagnosis until he had those results. With them, he could diagnose me and prescribe the correct medication for me, and help me with whatever this was.

It was very strange. For the first time ever I was comfy in a hospital. I was where I felt I should be. I felt I was unable to help myself until I knew what was going on. The doctor was coming to see me in the morning with all the documentation he needed to make a diagnosis.

I was not scared.

It was weird. I was excited.

I was discovering my next thing. While taking these tasty steroids, you don't sleep so well. That, combined with the snorers, made it a long, annoying night. At long last it was morning and I was learning the hospital's morning procedure. It was like a cross between the military, the flight attendants' safety routine during a flight, and staying in a hotel. I was used to all three - but not together.

I was told that the consultant would be in to see me around 11am. Mum and Sarah were going to be here at around 10.30am. This was good; I would have other people to hear what he said. At this stage I was too tired to take in any information, regardless of how important it might be. Having them there also meant I wouldn't need to repeat the conversation later, even if I could.

It was 7am. Hospital life started early. A lot was going on, but there was very little for me to do. I didn't mind a jot though, which was another new thing to me. Doing nothing and not caring. I was quite happy for the first time in my life to be doing nothing. But I was unable to shake the morning tiredness. Until these past few weeks I had always had the energy to spring out of bed, ready to get stuck into my day. But not these past few weeks. Why was that? Why was I so tired all the time and why was I unable to shake it?

I just lay in bed with my pet hate: the TV on in the background.

In my normal life I don't like television. I don't like the way it puts other people's thoughts and ideas in your head. You should be outside, experiencing the world first-hand. If you want a change of scenery, then change the scenery. Not the TV channel. Each and every one of your thoughts is a creation. Watching TV jams your creativity with whatever rubbish happens to be beamed out to you, the passive victim. Of course, in the hospital it's a bit different. I suppose I have to admit that for some people, it's a diversion from harder thoughts and fears and feelings.

Mum and Sarah appeared when they said they would. They had brought treats to make me feel better. Fresh fruit, chocolate, clean clothes etc. Hospitals are hopeless for chat. This is especially true when you're waiting to hear life-changing news. I had this feeling, though, that although I was the one in bed and I was the one who was having these problems, behind their smiles everyone was having a much worse time than I ever was. How unfair.

Let me recap the story so far, up to the point just before the neurologist came in by my bed. I just want to touch on the key areas that were all about to be brought together - I knew I had lesions on my brain from the results of my MRI a year before. I had very rapidly lost the use of my right leg and foot. For some reason, my vision dramatically deteriorated. Over these past two weeks I had started peeing the bed. My numb toes from a year ago had progressed into my body. It was numb from my neck down. To add to this list, I was also insanely dizzy. I came to feel as if I was going fall over, even when I was already lying down.

All of this was hand in hand with the most intense fatigue that this well-tested former Royal Marine had ever experienced.

The doctor walked into the room and came over to my bed and acknowledged my visitors. He had some friendly small talk with Mum and Sarah. He was relaxed. A total professional. He had news for us. He knew what was going on. And we were all waiting to hear what he had to say. He had the notes in his hand. My life, and my future - whatever that might be, were all in this clever man's hand. Everything I needed to know that would help me was here. I was to be told what was wrong with me. And I very badly needed to know.

Chapter 18 – The Puzzle Is Solved (2005)

"Paul, we are going to have to call this Multiple Sclerosis."

The consultant stayed with us at my bedside for a good half hour, answering all our questions. The news was affecting me differently from what you would probably imagine it would do. You would never imagine that you could be pleased to hear something like this. I had lived for two years with a mystery; a puzzle. I had the answer at last. My puzzle was no longer - and I was so glad.

This had been dragging on for the past 24 months as I had been slowly deteriorating. Understand, this was good news to me. I knew my enemy. I could see in front of me what I was about to fight. Don't get me wrong - this was about to be a fight and a half. And one hell of a learning curve – and I had such a lot to learn.

He left and we started to talk further. Mum went outside to make a phone call to my Dad. Sarah stayed with me. You would be astonished at how it was all being dealt with, calmly and with control. The worst thing that could have happened at this time was a lot of crying. Nothing good comes from crying at a time like that. Crying has its place. It's very important, but when you've hit a wall you must first try to focus. Then you must get it under control in the best way that you can. The crying can come later.

You know when you're in a tough place in hospital when visiting hours don't apply to you or your family. They can come when they wish, and they can go when they wish. This was one of those times. Mum and Sarah had been there for a long time talking and planning for getting me home. Dad appeared too. It was emotional, but no matter how weird this might sound, there was a bizarre feeling of relief, all round, for each of us. We all needed to take a step back. We had a lot to digest, but at last we had information.

Eventually, the three of them left. I have no idea how long they had been there, possibly for six or seven hours. It was late afternoon by the time Dad came. I was now alone, with too much time to think about things that I'd put into a 'too-hard' dark space in my mind.

In the early evening, a middle-aged nurse came into my room. I was lying in silence, looking at the ceiling, wondering how my life had brought itself to here. She asked me if I would like a bath. I spoke to her, teary but laughing at my own inability to deal with her question.

"It wouldn't be a good idea to put me in a bath. I was diagnosed with Multiple Sclerosis this morning - I imagine baths are dangerous for me!" She looked at me. She could tell exactly where

I was.

This was a lovely lady, caring and gentle. She came back with a wheelchair and told me that she had arranged a bath for me. She and a male nurse got me out of my bed and into the wheelchair. She then pushed me to the lift and we went up to the next floor and she wheeled me into a large room. The only thing that was in it was a massive bath with a funny little crane at the side. She pushed me over to the seat that was part of the crane. The two of us gradually moved me towards the seat. I took off my back-fastening gown. At long last I understood the purpose of these gowns. Easing me to the seat she strapped me to it, and using the electric controls, my nurse worked the crane and picked me up, swung me around, and nice and slowly, lowered me into the bath.

This had been my toughest day so far. Diagnosis in the morning, and then in the evening I was strapped to this seat and lowered into that bath. I am still so impressed with the way I was managed. It felt as if it was more than just a job to them. It was as if they really did care about me. With their efforts, they played such a big part in helping this young lad whom they didn't even know.

Chapter 19 – Going Home

The following day I was even less mobile but I had been booked to go back to the Royal Alexandra Hospital in Paisley. The neurologist had requested a couple of different tests to decide what strain of MS I had. Was it a relapsing remitting type of MS that you can live with? Or, was it the progressive type? Was it the type that would just keep coming at me until I died from it? I was yet to find this out, and these tests would tell us everything.

So here I was, back in the Royal Alexandra a year on, and heading back to the MRI machine for the second time. Every part of it was the same, only different. This time I was pushed in a wheelchair towards the Radiology Department. Yeah, it was familiar to me, but this time its purpose was critical. It wasn't as exciting to me as the year before, and it was certainly far more serious.

I wondered what they would find this time. It took three of them to get me out of the wheelchair and on to the same plastic sliding table. No Lynn though. Must have been her day off, or maybe she had seen my name on the list and chose not to be here. Could you blame her?

Anyway, the day went on. I was moved around to wherever I had to be. It was very well thought out. I didn't have to do a thing. I had my own ambulance and driver, and he knew exactly where to take me. I didn't care where I went. I wasn't bothered. I was pushed around, driven around, slid into big machines, had blood taken, swallowed pills. I was happy. I was away from my parents and Sarah and as far as I could tell that meant I could no longer upset them.

After a full day of tests I was taken back to Inverclyde Hospital, back to my bed, alone with my thoughts.

Mum and Dad were coming to see me again, and so was the neurologist. He had the results from the day's checks and would talk us through them. Another strange thing was going on. I was about to be told how likely it was that I would die from MS, whether this downward spiral was going to carry on. Was I about to be told that I was going to die?

When I look back on this doctor's visit it doesn't jump out as being the most intense of all. You would think it would be, but it wasn't. If the doctor had said: "Yes, you're going to go to sleep tonight and you'll not wake up", well, yes, I would have been sad. Sad for my parents, and Sarah, but that's all. I was unbearably tired. I had taken so much over the past two weeks that I wouldn't really have cared.

I don't think I was depressed. I was sad, yes, but not depressed. I had been riding on this path for long enough and that was that. I was not afraid. I felt I was just about capable of accepting anything, of accepting anything at all.

The consultant came in with my notes in his hand and sat with us again. According to Mum, this time he apparently gave us good news. I had no idea what was going on. Those few days remain a blur.

You see, at the time, I didn't have a clue about the different strains of Multiple Sclerosis. Why would I? I didn't even know what the previous day's further tests were. Mum and Dad were happy with what they heard, and therefore so was I.

I think a week passed and I got out of hospital, mentally prepared to step into my new world. A long and emotional period in hospital was finally over and it was now time to start to prepare for the next stage. Going home. I was taking my problem away with me, back to the life I'd once had. How would they fit together? Could they fit together?

What I do know about me is I was always the kid who could fit the square peg into the round hole.

Chapter 20 – Lying In Puddles

I was flat, mentally drained. I would just start to cry, and at any point. It was often when I was in the comfort of my Mum. The past few weeks had probably been tougher for her to deal with than for me. Mum came over to pick me up from the hospital and take me home. We were waiting for the ferry to cross the Clyde over to Dunoon. The weather was calm though very wet, a traditional west coast day. We were sitting in the queue when mum asked me about the fatigue.

"What is it like?" she said. I looked out at the rain and pointed over to a puddle. I explained to her: "I could quite happily go and lie in that puddle, not move, and go to sleep. I'd not care a jot."

It was tough for Mum, and I wish I had never said that.

I had travelled the world with the Marines and been to the Antarctic, but when the bombshell dropped, I faced a new world. At this point, I could relax with my Mum, but not easily otherwise.

My walking was still horrendous. In fact it was non-existent, so we just used my new found 'friend', the wheelchair. I would often wonder, when getting into the wheelchair, just how much I would rely on it in the future.

Until now, my only problems had been the cold or man-flu,

with the occasional Marine's broken bone. Admittedly a broken bone took its time to get better, and what was becoming obvious was – so was this. Was this possibly going to be it for me? I didn't know. This was starting to dominate my thoughts more and more.

Mum wanted to understand the things that she could see me experiencing, but couldn't identify with herself. She wanted to help. I know she would ask herself whether it was something she had or hadn't done when bringing me up. I knew that wasn't the case, but it was tough to watch her. I felt I had to apologise to her for this happening, as if it was possibly me who had done something wrong along the way.

I felt loved though. I was being cared for. Mum drove me back to my parents' house. Mum, Dad and Sarah had already agreed that this was the best place for me, for the first wee while. No one knew for sure, though. How do you plan for something you know nothing about? Imagine waking up and someone saying: "Go and pack. You're going on holiday." But then they refused to tell you what holiday you were going on. Was it trekking in the Antarctic or going windsurfing in Barbados? What should I pack? How much money will I need? We were all feeling our way in the dark, towards an uncertain future.

Every wee detail needed looking at, and from an angle I had no idea about. I couldn't even walk without help. I had been walking since I was ten months old and Mum was there for that. Here I was, again I didn't know how to walk.

Mum pulled into the drive of their house, Goldenlea. It was three miles out of Dunoon in Innellan, a quiet little place. I wasn't ready for people to see me. I was still too proud and still focusing on areas unknown to me. What really jumps out at me now is that I had, for the moment, 'wrapped on life'. The Bootneck again. It meant 'given up' on life. That wasn't me. But I had.

Anyway, Sarah and I moved into Goldenlea, where we planned to stay for a while until we came to terms with the situation. I had been good at adapting to new environments; it's a trick you learn in the Marines without really knowing you're learning it. This reality was different though. I had learned to endure hardship, yes, but hardships until now had always ended, and you went to the pub to reflect and unwind. Not this. I wanted to turn the page now and start a new chapter. The reality of this was starting to settle in for me. I had been diagnosed with Multiple Sclerosis and that was tough to swallow. But until now, believe it or not, I had been still experiencing an element of excitement, as I did when Dr Petty broke the MS news. But with most things in life, at some point, you revert back to your-self again. So, it was starting to come to me. This was it. I had this - I really had this!

Mum and Dad had gone all out to make us feel at home. For example, their front door bell is wireless, which meant it could be moved around the house to wherever. So they removed the doorbell and brought it into the bedroom for me, as a means of getting their attention. This was ideal and a service that I took great advantage of, to the point that they soon removed it from me and we reverted back to the traditional means of me phoning the house from my mobile to ask for another cup of tea. Adapt and overcome!

Chapter 21 - I'm Going To The Kitchen!

While all this had been going on, Mum had been phoned by her friend Brid McGahan, who at the time fronted an organisation called FATHOMS. This was a charity that used the local Professional Diving Academy's hyperbaric chamber to treat certain illnesses. Tom Brannan, who owned the Professional Diving Academy, or PDA, also rang Mum. It was explained that hyperbaric therapy was a proven method used to treat MS recovery after a flare up. Ideal!

I won't lie to you. I took a fair bit of convincing. I had MS and nothing can make it go away. There is no medication that can heal me. I will never be the same again.

But in the end I did get talked round. Boredom played a massive part in this. Also, I didn't seem to be as lethargic as before, so I agreed to go and visit it. It was a change of scenery if nothing else.

I was slowly becoming adjusted to getting in and out of the car or ambulances. You do learn and adapt to your situation. For example, I was now used to being the passenger and not the driver. People all around me were always bending over backwards to help me.

So, I ventured out to the PDA in Dunoon for my hyperbaric therapy. Getting there was a long, complex affair for all involved. I needed help getting dressed, and then more help moving around. Sure, the PDA was only four miles away from Goldenlea, but it meant me getting in and out of the car. I needed help from my parents and Sarah in every way, from putting my socks on to being at my side to act as my crutch when needed.

The PDA always had a lot of Marine-type individuals around it. Commercial divers and Marines are similar beasts. I was worried going up to the PDA because I was now disabled; in my eyes a cripple with MS. I thought I would be a laughing stock, not to my face, but maybe behind my back. I don't know why. None of my Marine mates were like that and a lot of them were also divers! For some reason I thought I would need to adopt bad attitude. Try and come across as a hard man.

Mum pulled up outside just as a group were leaving the building where the hyperbaric chamber was situated. My heart sank with embarrassment. Mum carried on the 'getting me out of the car' routine that we had become accustomed to. But this time it was different.

Before I had noticed, there were four diver students who had put their books and equipment down and they were helping this 55-year-old lady and her disabled son get out of the car.

No one was laughing at me. They were doing exactly what I would have done had I seen this going on in front of me. What's more, they were talking to me like a human being. They helped us right inside and to the room where the chamber was. They helped until they could help no more.

The chamber was cool. It resembled a massive fire extinguisher lying on its side with what looked like a fancy submarine-type hatch at the end for getting in and out. There were porthole windows to see into it, and inside the face masks you put on to breathe the oxygen. The excitement was ramped up with it requiring two people to operate it. One was there to work it and the other was there just in case something happened to the first operator - like a co-pilot in a plane.

Before going in the chamber I was told that I was being joined by another MS patient on this day, and this made me very nervous. I didn't want to speak with other people with MS. I didn't want to know their story. What if they had told me something worse than I was thinking? I now know that this was an impossibility, but my thoughts at the time were very flat, at rock bottom. However, she was about 65 and it was great to see her, as she was still going strong.

The way the chamber works is that you get in and close the door, which is also an air tight seal. The operators on the outside then pump air inside the now air-tight chamber. They keep doing this and the air pressure changes. It's just the same as a deep sea diver's experience when getting down into deeper sea. Brid advised us that oxygen helps the body heal, and we were being pressurised in the chamber to the equivalent pressure of being 33 feet under the water.

At this depth, the oxygen finds it easier to saturate the body. Under this pressure, the body's tissues relax, allowing the oxygen to speed up the healing process after an MS flare. It all seemed to make perfect sense to me and I was now actually becoming interested in what I was being told.

During this, the older lady turned to me and we started to talk about our lives. When I think about our first meeting it makes me laugh out loud. We were in the chamber for one hour. You do three 20-minute oxygen sessions in this time. Between each 20-minute session you take your mask off and breathe normally for five minutes. It's a safety measure. This allowed me to have a chat with the other people in there.

'Mary', the older woman, turned to me and said: "Paul, can I tell you something?" "Yes Mary, please do." "Paul, they say people with MS never truly smile again. I think it's true." Mary, if you have decided to read my book, can I please just apologise for bursting out laughing uncontrollably that day? I didn't mean to, but it was the perfect bit of humour I was looking for - and that I needed, thanks!

The first day I went into the chamber was a Monday. I had found it an exciting experience and, no disrespect to my parents' spare room, but it was just a cool change of scenery that also took up a large part of my day. I agreed I would do the next recommended 20 days of going in for one hour a day.

It was now Friday. Five days after I started going into the chamber and coming to the end of the fifth session. Before, if I'd looked at my toes and tried to move them, it was like looking at someone else's toes. I still had a sense of feeling in them though. Strangely, even though I couldn't move my foot or leg, when I woke up in the morning my body would just automatically stretch a perfect morning stretch. I couldn't understand it.

This Friday in the chamber I was staring at my toes and tried to give them a wiggle.

And they did!

What? I could wiggle my toes! I was shocked and delighted to the point that words failed me. This seems trivial now and probably also to you, but to me it was emotional. Funny, the moving of my toes, so small, but oh man so big! Neil Armstrong's words come to mind right now.

"That's one small wiggle of the toes for Paul! And a giant leap for the community!"

This was exciting. It released the same 'can do' attitude I had gained in the Marines before we did something physically hard. Admittedly, I developed this over the long period of commando training. At the start of training you have this 'I wonder if I can do' approach to what was coming. By the time training had finished, the 'I wonder' had been removed, to be replaced by an 'I CAN do' attitude.

Thankfully this mindset stays with you, and I was now benefiting from it more than ever.

I had just undergone a year of falling apart. I was noticing plenty going on with my body, and it was all negative. Parts of my own body were not doing what I naturally asked; everything I had noticed with myself during this time had been bad. Before, any success I had achieved in life was very much down to my body's great ability. I had, for the time being, completely lost this. But that day, in the chamber, I had moved my toes. This moved the goalposts in my favour.

I could move my toes. This was the first positive thing to happen to me, my body, in a year. Until this day it had been a gradual downhill slope. At the time I didn't realise the importance of this milestone.

Chapter 22 - Under Pressure (Hyperbaric Pressure)

Two weeks passed. For two long weeks I had been relying on others, while I was spending the majority of my time lying lazily in bed at my parents' house.

To add to my new challenge of having extreme vertigo, and my leg not working, was the fact that I was right handed - and now my right hand wasn't working either.

This was a tough one for reasons you wouldn't think of until it happens. Have you ever tried wiping your backside with your left hand? Until now I had never needed to think of such a weird challenge! You should try it. Or brushing your teeth with your left hand? You'll find that you can't do it as fast as you think you could. Or what about the unforeseen dangers of having a shave? Holy hell, talk about excitement. Don't try that one!

Sarah had bought me an electric razor and an electric tooth brush and I found out that they were for my birthday. It's my birthday? I had forgotten all about it amongst all the turmoil. Another gift was that Mum and Dad had put a plastic seat in the shower for me to sit on to get washed. Again, this was a strange thing to get used to - sitting in the shower.

Anyway, I was now starting to regain some energy and getting brassed off with this bed and room. I naturally started thinking: "I can move my toes, and I'm starting to be able to move my right foot again.

"I'M GOING TO THE KITCHEN!"

I had been building myself up to this for a few days; honestly, it was planned like a military operation. I was being slowly pulled out of the dark hole I was in. I was starting to think about stuff other than my body's failings. It was a big deal and I wanted to surprise everyone with this - going to the kitchen! The plan was in place, the time was now. I had to bite the bullet and take the 'step'.

I managed to get my legs out of bed and propped myself up with my left arm. In my pyjamas I awkwardly made my way over to the wall opposite, thankful that the door into the hall was on the same wall. I slowly made my way along the wall. I opened the door with my left hand – and there was the hall! It looked the same, though very different. From our bedroom to the kitchen seemed like the longest hall in the world, awash with obstacles; and to a former Royal Marine with MS, doing his '5 & 20s' risk assessments, it echoed DANGER all around.

To a normal healthy person, though, it is just a lovely hallway. It is tiled in black and white. The pattern of tiles was one big white one about a foot square, then a little black one about three inches square. They formed natural markers for my trek, you know, like the ones that mark your route on a hill walk. Tactically, I now had my markers and these became a gauge for my efforts along the hallway.

Every step was a challenge. After each challenge I would stop and debrief myself. I would then plan moving forward to the next black tile, and reflect on it once I reached it. I did this with each step I took. Each step was tough, but I focused on making each one bigger. If the step was a good one, I would give myself a good old fashioned 'chuck up' (Bootneck for compliment); on the other hand, if it was nonsense then I would put myself down with constructive criticism, military fashion: "That was crap PK, get your finger out and stop loafing."

So I started my 5 & 20 metre risk assessment. By now I had mentally planned the assault or, if you like, the move to the kitchen. This was going to be tough, but I had my plan in place. The Marines had taught me a lot and my commando training was standing firmly by me. Remember Paul, if this all goes pear-shaped mate, revert instantly to the basic plan. That's what it's there for buddy! The basic plan being: man, just get to the kitchen!

The pictures on the walls were my first obstacles. Some were hand painted for Mum by her close friend Pauline. The others were photos of our family; one was a cracker of my nephews climbing a tree - 'good effort lads! Remember always to keep three points of contact with the tree. OK?'

One picture in particular that sticks out in my memory, and

is still in the hall, is a black and white photo of my Papa - my Dad's Dad - standing outside his shop in Glasgow back in the 1930s. Papa had died before I was born, so I had never met him, though he was here now, watching me learn to walk for the second time in my life.

Off I went. It could be described as jumping into a river and hoping that it's deep enough, something I was cognisant with, so I had the guts to take the plunge.

It was going well. I was now negotiating the left corner with the glass cabinet with loads of my late Nana's Wedgewood. Mum loves Nana's Wedgewood. If I had taken out the cabinet I would have been in trouble, possibly even hospital again. Centrifugally, it was all against me. But determination, and Papa on the wall watching over both me and now Nana's Wedgewood, got me round it. The final five-metre straight to the kitchen was in sight. The kitchen and a well-earned seat were my motivation and reward.

I was doing well; momentum was on my side; although the risk assessor in me was considering momentum a double-edged sword that could cut me at any moment.

Finally, I got to the kitchen door to be met by both parents - with a look of shocked horror on their faces.

"Well, that went well", I said, with a big smile on my face. I was delighted with the effort I had just made.

I met silence and raised eyebrows.

I turned and looked up the hall to where they were staring. There were pictures lying on the floor, a couple squint but still on their hook, and hand prints on the glass cabinet, with a couple of pieces of Nana's Wedgewood lying on their sides, still rocking.

"Ah" I eventually said. "Nothing's broken, not even a finger." This was success and the start of something great!

Chapter 23 – Fartlek

The moving of my toes in the hyperbaric chamber that day was all I had needed to lift my confidence and to start thinking of the future and not reliving the past. What I had been considering a worry, I now considered a manageable, if tough, unknown goal.

It's strange how a shift in mind-set can change your course of thinking, and, ultimately your doing. Going from not being able to move my toes, to being able to move them, proved a lot to me. Where could this lead? Will this - can this - carry me forward? I thought 'yes' without hesitation.

Over these years I have found one thing to be true. It is hard to police and keep control of but I can assure you - what you think about, you really do bring about. The problem is, it is very easy to think about the things you don't want to recall, especially in today's world. Worry just seems to be a part of modern life for many people.

So, back to the road in front of my parents' house. I was becoming more mobile. I could now walk up to 100 metres without having to stop for a rest. Don't get me wrong, it was not pretty but I didn't care. I was doing it. I had my leg brace. I had the training ground of the road in front of my parents' home, and I was visiting the hyperbaric chamber every day.

I was coming to the end of the second of four weeks of going in the hyperbaric chamber daily; I was pushing myself hard. Fitness, mental and physical, was my main focus. It was all I would allow myself to think about. Getting better. Not getting worse. Again it was a focus that was tough to maintain.

How, when you are just constantly getting bad news, can you stay positive? Never give up, grasp what you can, even if it's just moving your toes. And then as you succeed with each step, don't rest on your laurels. Move on, reach the next tile in the hallway.

Mum and Dad were amazing. Our time at Goldenlea was a real blessing. It was perfect for what we needed at this time. Sarah and I had been here for a few weeks now, and I was slowly improving. I could walk the 100 metres. I was not focusing on going further than this, I was instead focusing on getting my technique together, and then I would start to push the distance again.

For this, I was going to revert to a training session I had used in the Marines called 'Fartleking'. It comes from a Swedish word that means 'Speed Play'. Fartlek provides an excellent endurance and strength session, as well as helping to improve your speed and your personal awareness. It allows you to work at speed training, but with recovery breaks.

Before, I would use this for sprinting for a distance of three lamp posts apart, and then jogging for two to get my breath back. A watered-down version of this trick was going to stand me in good ground. I could make the adjustment to how hard or easy I wanted it to be and over what distance I fancied. Again, I made my past my helper, not my foe.

Sarah and I looked at our position and we agreed that it was time to move back into Sarah's house.

Something that I didn't mention, and really should have, is that during my time in hospital we agreed to give Kyle away.

We knew a lady who had been looking for a dog. She could give him all that he needed. There was no way we could have kept this now full-sized Collie puppy. He had too much energy for our new situation, and he had been used to the freedom of running around a farm. I could never have exercised him enough. Sarah had her hands full with her work and now me. It was so sad for us. But at the time, it was required.

We had no idea what the future held for me. We had to try to be realistic about that too. I still see him from time to time. He has no idea who I am, sad but hey, he's happy, and that's enough to make me smile.

So Sarah and I moved back into Maymor, her house in town. I didn't realise it at the time, but this was going to be harder for me than I had ever thought it could have been.

A number of changes were being made in my life - the whole

hyperbaric chamber thing, regular contact with my GP, and I had also started to visit Dunoon Hospital to the physiotherapist to be stretched. Actually I don't think 'a number of changes' really quite cuts it. My life was now completely different. But for now 'new' was fine. New was vibrating under this level of intensity, and that was keeping me occupied and my thoughts busy.

Going home to Sarah's was tough. I don't quite know how to tell this and get the feeling across, but it was going right into the heart of my old life for the first time; a house full of things I had bought for my lifestyle and personal use. A life I had loved so much. I didn't realise it, but the effect this would have on me was going to be so much worse than I could ever have imagined.

Many levels of adjustment had been required already to get me here, but nothing we'd achieved had really prepared me for this. You think you can plan for things, but for some things there can be no planning. The family couldn't have gone in before me and removed my windsurfing equipment, my climbing harness, my snowboard. That stuff was personal to me.

Sarah brought me back to the house. She hadn't really been home in the past few weeks either. Between running around after me while holding down her full-time job, she had only the time to nip in and feed the cat when passing on her way to

Goldenlea.

So slowly, and with great physical and mental difficulty, I walked up the three steps to the front door. And went in.

The first thing I met was my pair of Scarpa mountain boots at the door. These were the ones I had bought when I was at ProAdventure and wore at Quadmania. They were next to Kyle's rubber squeaky bone. It used to drive me up the wall the way he would jump around with it, hyperactive, over and over and over. Why did I used to get annoyed with him? He was just being a pup; I did know he was now in a better place for him than being here with me though.

I cracked on further into the house, trying to settle back in and get things the way they now needed to be.

Sarah was bringing things in from the car and I was slowly and unsteadily walking around the house, not really knowing what to do to help her. It was upsetting me. Seeing all my old stuff, the stuff that I loved; my wakeboard just looked back at me when I saw it. I went into the kitchen and looked out to the back garden. There was my wetsuit hanging over the back wall and my four windsurfing boards propped up next to it.

I became so upset that day that Sarah phoned my parents, asking them to help us. They thought fast of how to approach our problem. My brother-in-law Euan, who had been my friend before he had met my big sister Nicola, jumped at their suggestion and phoned me.

He told me he had taken the next day off work and he was going to pick me up at four in the afternoon. We were taking the car and going on a road trip, heading up north-west towards Fort William, to get me out of Dunoon.

It was perfect. I needed to get away and with an old friend. Euan and I headed off. It was brilliant and just what the doctor ordered. I couldn't really walk, but the beauty of Fort William, amongst other things, is you can get to the top of mountains in cable cars. And that's what we did.

It was a great getaway and a tiny view of my old life, but from a different angle. It was a valuable lesson, as well as a much-needed escape. I was learning more than ever before: regardless how empty the glass may appear, there is always more in it.

Chapter 24 – If You Can't Walk, You Can't Drink

We headed back to Dunoon after a great night away up there, doing nothing but talking and eating and very little walking. It was my first real taste of normality since the rapid decline of the months and weeks before. Euan had spoken with a couple of our other friends and it was arranged that we would meet up that night, back in Dunoon. I was feeling more sociable now. It was a Friday, after all, and I was enjoying the shift into relative normality that we had just had.

Euan came for me at Sarah's house that night. We were on foot as we were only going on what to a healthy guy was a five minute walk into town. I was still finding the back garden full of windsurfing equipment tough to look at; but I was dealing with it. Sarah had also arranged to go out that night with her friends and we would meet after and swap stories. I imagine she needed a night out to forget the scene with me, possibly more than I needed my social break.

By the time I had walked down to the town I was bit of a mess. This five minute walk had taken Euan and me 30 minutes. And I now had a horrendous limp. But we went into Sinbad's pub in the town centre for my first pint in a crowd for months.

I walked in to this busy pub. Euan had by this point gone in front of me and was being my front leading crutch. I was dragging my left leg quite badly. Even though I had my leg brace on, it had been a tough hour leading up to getting in here. I followed Euan into the pub full of people I knew. Michelle the barmaid came round the bar and came up close enough to my face so I could hear her. She pointed right in my face and shouted so I could hear above the music: "PK, if you can't walk, you can't drink."

Michelle was just doing her job. She had come up to me in her firm but fair manner to let me know I had had enough to drink. Euan took her aside and had a quiet word in her ear, while Jasper came over and took over Euan's role as my crutch. The next thing I knew, Michelle came over all apologetic and embarrassed with one pint after the next. I don't think I paid for a drink that night. Every cloud has a silver lining.

Finally, the night was over. Now I couldn't walk at all. And I certainly couldn't drink.

I was still sober, I thought, but my body had well and truly gone to sleep. This was my first experience of a night out on the town with MS. I asked Euan and Jasper to take me home. I now felt as if I had taken this night as far as I wanted it to go. The two of them were no longer simply my crutch. I couldn't walk at all. We got a taxi up the road. Again, this required telling the driver that I was not that drunk. I had drunk just three pints of lager.

Euan and Jasper got me home safely. They then made sure that

I was safe and could handle myself once they left. I don't know, but I imagine they went back down to the pub. I know I would have.

I was now home alone for the first time, tipsy, and surrounded by memories from my past. I could not walk. I could not crawl. I dragged myself from room to room. I tried to go about my usual get 'ready for bed' routine - getting undressed, drinking a glass of water. But my body was now as fast asleep as it had ever been before, only I was very much awake.

I was becoming incredibly frustrated and irate. I was upset at being like this and alone. The situation was infecting my mood. For the first time I was becoming angry. I was livid at my own body. I was starting to hate it, truly hate it. I didn't just hate my body, I actually despised it.

I made my way into the toilet to use it before I went to bed. I had to drag myself with one arm, my left arm at that. I couldn't get myself up to use the toilet. I was naked, so I rolled into the bath. I lay in the bath and had a lying down pee that also ended up all over me. I was now even more upset. This was not me. It can't be me. Something was sinking in and admittedly it was sinking in at the wrong time. It slowly dawned on me that this body actually was not 'me'; it was my body, yes, But it was not me. I was just trapped in this broken body.

I fell out the bath and slowly (yet as fast as I could) worked my way into the hall. I crawled over to the coat hangers and propped myself up against the wall as best I could.

I was now raging. I angrily looked around at what I could blame. I pulled the first thing I could get a hold of. A coat hanging up on the wall-mounted coat hanger was the first thing I ripped it off the wall.

I then systematically made my way around the house smashing up everything I could reach.

In our bedroom I even managed to upturn our bed, and pulled over the wardrobe. That was a tough one for me. I had to move it away from the wall with one hand while lying down. I squeezed in behind it and then with one arm pushed against it and the wall, rocking it until it eventually toppled. What a great achievement. I was so proud at what I was still able to do.

If I could reach it, it was pulled over or smashed. I then lay in silence in the now destroyed house, but admittedly destroyed only from waist height down, and only because I couldn't get any higher.

Something was still annoying me. I lay on the floor looking at my naked, broken body. I was disgusted with it. I wanted it to know how much it had failed me. How angry and upset it had now made me. It had carried me through my life's proudest times from the physical heights of being a Royal Marine Commando, to this. I thought about this next idea. I calmly put my fingers down my throat and wiggled them around and finally vomited on myself. I moved my head around to make sure I got it all. I was finally satisfied. I looked at my work and smiled while crying at what a disgusting thing I had done.

This was the start of the next massive turning point for me. I had experienced first-hand how the body and the mind can be at two different places. People forget this. You are only living in your body, I promise. It is your 'meat suit'. For me, this was a time where I started thinking: "Yeah it might be my body that's broken, but not my soul." That will never break. I might have been upset and angry that night, but my mind was still not broken!

I pulled together some of the clothes I had angrily thrown around the house, crawled under them and went to sleep.

Chapter 25 – The Morning After

I woke. It was morning. Sarah had come home from her night out and found me and the house like this. She had checked that I was still alive, and then she cleaned up the house as well she could, considering it was 1am in the morning, and she too had been out with her friends.

She woke me on her way out to work. I told her I would have the house cleaned that day. For some reason I wasn't as pleased with myself that morning as I had been the night before. Smashing the place up had been a much quicker and easier affair, but it gave me some focus for that day and, admittedly, I called in help from poor Mum for the final touches. It was another thing my Mum could probably have done without seeing. Her broken child, being this distressed and disturbed.

Later that day I decided to take the until now five-minute nip down the town for some more Ibuprofen. I was still getting wild nerve pains around this buckled body, but Ibuprofen was, and still is, a good help, taking the edge off the pain I was becoming ever more used to living with.

I had cleaned the house as well as Mum and I could manage. I got myself ready for popping down to the town to the pharmacy. I put my leg brace on, and mentally prepared to step into the now-dangerous big and fast world. It took me two hours to get to the chemist. There was a lot of stopping and sitting on walls along the way, just soaking up the world. It's cool that when things change, so can you - if you allow it. I started to appreciate simple things.

Like breathing the fresh Dunoon sea air.

Just taking a seat on a wall or bench.

Stopping and soaking up my surroundings.

Having a chat with an older person who was doing the same as me.

I eventually made it to the chemist and carefully and slowly went in and up to the counter. Shops had also become a nightmare. I was discovering along the way that shops can make me nervous and walking at other people's speed is hard.

I handed in my prescription and then made my way over to the seat in the corner while it was prepared. I was sitting reflecting on the interesting night I had just experienced. I was making a damned big effort not to feel sorry for myself and I was wondering how I could ever apologise enough to Sarah. I knew she didn't need me to but I wanted to anyway.

I decided that I had done enough thinking for the day; I had to bring my focus back on to making my body work.

While there and deep in these thoughts, a drug addict came walking in - perfectly - and went over for his daily drink of methadone. He drank this down into his (as far as I could tell) perfect body. I sat there and watched him leave. I now know that my feelings that day were not fair. I didn't know this guy. I didn't know what his life experiences had been. I could not judge him from my own life's point of view. That's not accurate or fair on him. That day, and for a good while after, I was angry with what I had seen and experienced; but I'm not now.

Chapter 26 – All At Sea

I was still adjusting to my life's dramatic change; walking around not really knowing what was going on. Mentally, I felt numb, not knowing much about anything any more. This did take some time to get used to, months and months actually; to the point that even though I was insanely tired I hated going to sleep, going to sleep meant waking up and having to readjust to the news over again each day.

I decided on one particular day to make my way round to a flat I had bought from my family when my grandparents had died years before. There was no real reason for going here other than boredom I suppose. It was round the corner from Sarah's house and only maybe 500 metres away. A short distance to a healthy person I know, but it had recently become the perfect distance for me to start and try and walk to. The plan was that I would limp to Jacksonville and then sit by myself and recharge ready for the walk back. Unknown to me, it turned out that this walk was going to make a momentous and positive difference.

After the short walk I finally made it to Jacksonville from Maymor and went into the house for the seat I had been looking forward to. I had many fond memories of Jacksonville from growing up. I had been close to my grandparents and would often stay the night with them. They had Benjy, a toy poodle that was full of positive and endless energy, we would tire each other out before bed time.

This visit mentally took me back to that time in life; a time of feeling safe without a serious care in the world, basically the way I had felt when under the care of my grandparents. As if no harm could ever come to me.

I put on the stereo. It was a CD player that I was given many years before as a birthday present, and like all old furniture and technology it had been demoted in importance over time so was now living in Jacksonville as part of the furniture as I was getting the flat ready to rent out. The CD player already had a Jamie Cullum CD in it; and a song came on called All at Sea.

I listened to the words to that song so intensely that day; it was like honey to my ears:

I'm all at sea

Where no-one can bother me

Forgot my roots

If only for a day

Just me and my thoughts sailing far away

Like a warm drink it seeps into my soul

Please just leave me right here on my own

Later on you could spend some time with me

If you want to

All at sea

I'm all at sea

Where no-one can bother me

I sleep by myself

I drink on my own

Don't speak to nobody

I gave away my phone

Like a warm drink it seeps into my soul

Please just leave me right here on my own

Later on you could spend some time with me

If you want to

All at sea

I had started to cry; I mean really cry and wouldn't and couldn't stop. I didn't feel I should stop though, I felt it best to just cry. This crying felt like it was making a difference, and that it was making me feel better. It was purely for my benefit; no one else was there, only me. I cried until the song finished, when I would then play it again and then again. I cried like I had never cried before, as if someone very close had just left me. I didn't know it at the time but someone had - the old me, and this was me mourning. As far as I was concerned I was saying good bye to the old me.

I stayed in Jacksonville listening to Jamie Cullum's All at Sea over and over and over. I believe I cried myself to a better place that day. Without knowing it, I was acclimatising and preparing myself to be able to step into my now different future. Back to being me, a guy ready to take on the world again.

Chapter 27 – Why Not?

After a few weeks I had moved this walking caper up a notch to tackle the road in front of Goldenlea. I had been to see my GP. He had prescribed a brace for my right leg, and I had been over to Inverclyde Hospital to have it fitted, and this really helped my foot drop. Foot drop is when you cannot lift or point your foot up the way. With foot drop, your toes act like the stopper on a roller skate. Makes walking tricky.

A couple of weeks passed with some intense training. Finally, I called Sarah and my parents to watch me in front of the house. They still laugh now at the time I said: "Look, look! I'm almost back to walking normally!" Little did I know I was far from it. But to me it was enough to boldly say to the family: "This time next year, I'm going to do the UK 24-hour Three Peaks Mountain Challenge", something I would have considered a tough one as a fit serving Marine. In my mind: "Why not?"

This was to become my big thought, a challenge, and a focus. I had decided to set my sights high, and go for it. The Three Peaks 24-hour Mountain Challenge: Mount Snowdon, the highest mountain in Wales, then straight into a drive to Scafell Pike, the highest mountain in England, and then a final drive to the last mountain, the UK's highest, Ben Nevis in Scotland. This was where you went for the mad dash to the summit. All this in 24 hours. I had decided to do this the following year.

But first we'll learn to walk again, PK.

Chapter 28 – Bottoms Up!

The hyperbaric chamber at the PDA had made such a difference over the 20 days of going into it. It was proof that there were things that could help me. I had been advised that MS was a condition where your own immune system attacks your nerve system. The nerve system has a protective cover called the myelin sheath. The myelin sheath is the same as the insulation around an electric cable. It keeps the electricity protected and in the cable. No myelin sheath, and then the nerve is unprotected and the message doesn't get to where it is meant to be going. In very bad cases, the MS can even chew its way right through the nerve and, well, that's that.

Apparently though, gluten in your diet weakens the myelin sheath. If you remove gluten from your diet the myelin sheath becomes tougher and this then helps with MS. A tougher myelin sheath means better protection for your nerves. Have you ever tried a gluten free diet? In today's world this is a tough one. However after hearing about it, I started on a diet of gluten-free food.

I was on a gluten free diet, I was visiting the hyperbaric chamber, and I was pushing myself harder with walks than I had ever done before. I was doing everything to help my situation. I get asked often: "What do you think has been the main thing that helped you?" It's very hard to put my thoughts on that across without sounding like a knob. I did so much that I couldn't do more. I changed my diet. I visited the hyperbaric chamber regularly; I was going out for walks every day until I couldn't walk any more.

I even booked into a retreat for a week's detox. There I ate nothing but volcanic clay for seven days and had two colonic irrigations a day. It was a hard yet hilarious seven days.

I have to share a story with you that just defies normality and is humour at the lowest level.

The week of the detox it had been explained that we would be doing two colonic irrigations a day as well as eating nothing but this volcanic clay. To keep things more relaxed and personal we used a system called a colonic board.

The colonic board allowed you to do your own colonics when you wanted. You used this in your own en suite toilet of your apartment. You laid the board over your toilet and then just positioned yourself lying down on the board which had a big angled hole at the relevant end. You put a wee nozzle about an inch into your back side. You had a wee tap on a hose that was attached to the nozzle. Open the tap up and the water runs in. Fill yourself up and eventually it floods back out. Super clean - for now!

No joke, it was very straight forward and well thought out. These colonics took around 45 minutes. Once you were finished you lay there for a further five minutes to ensure all the water was out.

It was winter at the time. I went into my toilet and set the system up. I filled my quota of water up into the system's bucket, which was high up. Gravity forced it through - all of it.

I always opened the roof window for a good flow of air into the room. Because it was winter I turned up the heater to full blast to keep it warm for the 45 minutes of having the window open.

It was ready. Bucket full of water, window open, heating pumping full bore, colonic board in place over the loo. So I lay on it and did my 45 minute of colonic irrigation. The water was finished and I was, as far as I could tell, 'empty'.

The bathroom had a lovely tied floor. I climbed off the board quite happy with how it had all gone. When standing up a load more of my waste and water fell out my backside onto the floor behind me. I turned in shock. Aw man! It's ok though, no big deal, it's tiled floor. I'll clean this up in no time. I'll use a towel to get the most of it cleaned up and I'll secretly throw it in the rubbish bin outside, then I'll get the rest with toilet paper.

I got the towel off the towel rail. Still stark naked I bent over to start and clean it up. But my bum kissed the roasting radiator I had put on an hour before. I uncontrollably jumped forward with fright and a burnt backside, and landed naked, standing with both feet in my own shite. There was only one thing left I could do. Laugh hysterically.

Chapter 29 – Enter Zander (July 2006)

Over the years I have found that life presents me with what I need, when I need it and in the strangest way. I have held back telling you about an area of my life that instantly made the difference, and at a time when it was most required. It has been such an important part that it requires its own chapter.

I would like to introduce you to Zander.

I will try and tell you how important he is in my life. But to be honest, before I have even written them, I can tell you right now that my words won't come close. The best way I can think to put it across is that the second he was born; he became number one, my motivation and now my focus.

Not long after Sarah and I had moved back into Maymor from my parents' house, life was in turmoil but we were going with it, and then we were thrown a scary curve ball.

Sarah was pregnant. That was scary. But now that miraculous little baby has become our wonderful little boy. He is the core of my life.

This is why I'm struggling to explain it.

To that point, we hadn't had to think about anyone other than ourselves. Now we were engulfed with uncertainty.

How could we have let this happen? What appalling timing. Or was it? We don't feel ready to accept this. How will we cope?

The list went on and on and, well, so did life. As John Lennon said: "Life is what happens when you're busy making other plans."

Sarah would help anyone in any situation. She is quiet, strong, and with the ability to trust but not be fooled. Looking back it's now obvious that the areas where I was weak she was strong, and vice versa. This teamwork stood us in good stead, especially when we didn't know what lay ahead.

In the past I have often said 'yes' when I probably should have said 'no' because of not really knowing how it was going to work out. But together Sarah and I would think about it and somehow get away with it. I can now see that this is what happened here too. I had my usual 'no cuff too tough' head on and Sarah went straight into her 'we need to think about this and plan, Paul!' routine.

Looking back, I don't think the shit was yet again hitting the fan. It was serious, yes, but at the other end of the spectrum. Any previous feelings at this level I had experienced had been destructive, uncontrollable and limited to me. But this – this was constructive, and had a wider impact than just on me. I would soon learn it would be far more powerful than anything I had experienced in the past couple of years.

For the time being I was back at Quadmania, but not teaching.

I know I was there getting my life back on track, as well as I could. I was finding it tough, both physically and mentally.

I had been given the job when I was a healthy instructor, and to fill a company management role. I was now unable to do all that I had been employed to do, and this was annoying me. Sarah was pregnant, and I wasn't fulfilling my workplace role. My life required a completely different approach that only I could put into place. This meant that I would also need to take a totally new approach to my life, well our lives really, and now there was about to be three of us.

It was four months after my diagnosis and the lowest point of my breakdown. My walking was much better, but only for short bursts of a mile or so. I had either become used to my lower energy level or it had improved. I've never really been too sure with that one. I was on steroids a lot of the time and a number of other 'wee' problems had developed along the way. I now had a urine bag strapped to my leg for example.

I had been thinking about this long and hard over the previous couple of months while I was back working at Quadmania or, more likely, giving the appearance of working.

I had decided that the only way to go forward proudly was to go into business for myself. I discussed it with Dad, took advice, and had meetings with friends of the family who had their own business.

Sarah and I had decided not to find out the baby's sex. I can only describe it as feeling the parcels of your presents at Christmas. Something I had never done. If the people wanted you to know what you were getting why would they wrap it up?

We went to every pre-natal class that was going and listened to others who had just been through the birth of a first baby. My older sister Nicola and her husband Euan had had their babies Lewis and Rory only the year before. So Nicola was well up on the whole situation and happy to discuss it with Sarah.

We had decided that our baby would be born in the Southern General Hospital. Yes, the same hospital where I had been given my lumbar puncture.

I was completely wrapped up in Sarah. It was her time now to be the supported person. I was only too glad to be there for her. We were sharing the very best time of our lives together.

It was now two weeks past our child's due date. It had been decided that it would be best if Sarah was induced. It was my turn to hang around and be supportive; something I was delighted to do. They gave Sarah the pills that triggered the induction and then I was advised there was nothing more I could do, so would I please leave and come back tomorrow morning at 10am.

I wasn't expecting this, and I felt really quite unimportant. I phoned Liam and Janie, my old friends who luckily lived nearby the hospital and asked if I could possibly crash on their couch.

That night we went out for a drink. Sarah had been fine when I had left and seemed quite happy with me being with these friends. Liam and Janie were old friends who I had not seen for a while. We discussed both the hard time I had been having with MS, but mainly the exciting time I had ahead of me. At the time, Liam and Janie didn't have kids either, though they now have Kel and Anna.

Sarah was sending me a rather different tone of text messages as the evening went on. They were noticeably going downhill. By about 9pm I was getting messages along the lines of 'this is really stinging me now'. And by 6am the following day they were more like 'you keep your bloody hands off me in future, Paul Kerr'.

I bought a coffee and a bacon roll, and felt pretty relaxed and confident before I headed back to the hospital that morning. However, I wasn't expecting to see her the way she was. It knocked the wind out of me. She was on the floor rocking back and forwards with her sweaty phone in hand, a soaking brow, and a very red and tired face. I had got it wrong. There was, and still is, guilt. I had been out with friends the previous evening and then had a lovely night's sleep at theirs. She, on the other hand, had a night's work to do.

It was a long day for Sarah and a very emotional one for me too. She was a true hero. She had only gas and air. Then at 6.30 that evening a wee baby boy arrived - and words cannot begin to tell you how I felt.

We had talked about different names before he was born. But we both knew instantly that our Zander was here. It was as if he had always been called Zander, and it was as if he had always been ours.

I instantly became number two in our team. It was where I wanted to be then, and I've gladly been there ever since. I didn't really matter as much any more. I had to provide; I had to be here to bring up my Zander as well as I could. I had always had drive and I had always had focus, but this brought both to a whole new level.

Zander and me swimming the Clyde with Davie Robertson giving his loyal kayak support

Chapter 30 – Proform Marine

Eventually, Proform Marine Ltd was also born. I had it planned. Proform Marine was to become a small boat service operating in and around the River Clyde. I was going to offer powerboat training or safety cover if required. This could have been for divers, or civil construction. It's what I knew well and loved. Small boat driving had also been what I had done when I was in the Marines, so it made sense to focus on that. Mainly, it was based around me and my past lifestyle. It allowed me to push as hard as I wanted and arrange my day to suit myself and in the way that I now needed to do.

I started to look around for a RIB (Rigid hull Inflatable Boat) and to start with I was looking for one with a small cabin and a compact bed too (if such a thing even existed). This was so that I could get an hour's sleep at lunch time. At that time I couldn't have worked 9 to 5, five days a week. My day now felt as if it should have ended at 11am. I thought about it and decided if I could have a wee sleep for an hour at lunchtime, when my clients were away for their lunch, then I could get away with appearing to them to be a man of normal fitness. Also, I could be anywhere around the Clyde with my RIB, so I would be self-sufficient while providing a worthwhile service. It all seemed a workable plan.

I discussed it with Euan, my brother-in-law, who was in business for himself. He advised me to go out and get some clients around the Clyde and then take my 'proof of requirement' to the bank. I knew that a new RIB company, the same as a car breakdown service, had just launched in the Clyde called Clyde Sea Recovery (CSR). I thought they might be looking for some part-time help and assistance so I went into visit them at their office at the Holy Loch Marina, just outside Dunoon.

Taking these steps was hard for me; not just physically, but also ridiculously mentally challenging. I could get away with walking normally now for maybe 400 metres before I started to limp and walk like a drunken guy.

I now had a catheter bag strapped to my leg for urinating without my control; I had a fully mobile, but numb, body and I was on steroids to help me through the day. The point is that I could appear to be normal while standing for a limited time. If I could just get a seat though, regardless of where I was sitting, I could function perfectly.

I made my way out to the Holy Loch Marina and found where the Clyde Sea Recovery office was. I walked into their office to introduce myself. I recognised the woman at the front desk but couldn't place her. I introduced myself and told her why I was there. She told me that I had taken she and her family out quad biking at Quadmania a year before; strangely, I did remember that particular trek amongst a possible thousand treks that year.

I asked, while standing unaided – with my mobility clock now ticking – if there was anyone around to talk to me about being a service provider. She told me that Brendon, her husband and the owner of CSR, was out on the water in the CSR RIB. I gave her my business card and asked if she would have him call me.

When I was getting back into the car I saw a couple of people walking towards the CSR office. They were dressed in RIB type clothing and carrying helmets. I went over and asked if one of them was Brendon. A very switched-on and friendly individual put his hand forward and introduced himself as Brendon Wallace. We had a two minute chat about why I was there and I told him that Rachel had my business card. I could see that he was busy, and I let him get back to his day, asking him please to feel free to call me.

I immediately liked both Brendon and Rachel. You know that feeling you get right from the start when meeting someone new, when there are no question marks over the first encounter.

A couple of days later I was called by Brendon who said that he would like to talk business with me, and asked if Sarah and I would like to go for dinner at their house that weekend. It was a phone call that I was not expecting. But it certainly interested me!

Over the course of that dinner, Brendon said that the person he had earmarked to move to Dunoon and work for CSR was now unable to do it. If I liked, I could take a desk in their office and push Proform Marine whilst giving CSR my time when required. He said that I would be paid a retainer every month for doing so, and the office would be rent free. This was the start to a valuable friendship. I am now the godfather of Jaydon, their youngest child.

A second, and again unexpected, phone call that week was from Tom Brannan, one of the owners of the Hyperbaric Chamber and the Professional Diving Academy. Tom had heard on the grapevine that I was buying a RIB and was would be offering training courses. It so happened he was about to introduce a RIB driving course to the diving courses they already offered at the PDA, and could I pop in and discuss it with them.

That was a very interesting week and a great and further example of my mantra: what you think about, you bring about. My view on the world, and how it really works, was changing right in front of me. My world too was changing. I felt that I was given opportunities I would not have even dared hope for.

I was probably taking a lot of risks and steps into the unknown, but why not? The way I was viewing life was that I had just gone through a tough time. What more could happen? I wasn't just randomly taking gambles. I was planning my moves. In fact I was planning more deliberately than I had ever done before. I valued life more than ever before. I wasn't looking back at yesterday; I was becoming tuned into the greater excitements of tomorrow.

I still look back on the day that Mum and Dad stood round my bed waiting for Dr Petty to announce what my strain of MS was. Was I going to live? Or was I going to die? Do you know anyone else who has been waiting to hear such news and then be partially handed back their life like that? It changes your views on things. It puts a whole new edge on the statement 'let's give it a go, and see what happens'.

Chapter 31 – Highs And Lows

Proform was going well. The business was doing a good bit of work in the Clyde and I was loving this new experience of being involved in business. Yes, it was a challenge, but something I was up for learning about along the way. I was enjoying driving it forward. The purpose that was forcing me out of bed in the morning was brilliant. I didn't fully realise at the time, but this vital part of my day was now a vital part of my life, and very much continues to be. It was forcing some more normality back into my life, whether I liked it or not. Until then I hadn't even realised I was missing it. It was just another aspect of day-to-day living that I hadn't noticed had gone but was now back; another area that demanded that I think about things other than how I felt, and which required me to be as physically normal and healthy as I could be; it was ideal.

I can now look back and say there were some astronomical mistakes along the way, but thankfully a lot of success too. I am not talking about success on a financially grand scale. I would land a job for the company and we would then go forward and make it work. Yes, business was - and still is - a sharp learning curve; I suppose a bit like school. You have work to do, you plan it out and go forward and do it. At the end of the day if your effort wasn't good enough the teacher, or in this case the client, would let you know.

So generally things were going well. I was always looking for the next opportunity to take business to the next level of operation though. I was going on courses and reaching out for the next contact and opportunity to move on.

I had been asked to go down south for a business meeting with a ship security company looking to put security teams on ships at sea. I had met the man who invited me to this meeting around year before, when I'd been on a course where he was the instructor. Passing this course would give me the qualifications to get into the managerial side of maritime security. I realised I could shape this to be a total desk job, working with a lad I knew from my past.

It was my understanding that I was not to be out as one of the operatives so, as far as I was concerned, my health problem didn't matter a jot. I was walking normally and the role I would be playing in the team was to be office-based organising the teams. This was work that my Marine background was going to be perfect for.

So me, and one other who was also going to be on the team, travelled from Glasgow down south in his car. It was an exciting time, the plan was a good one; I liked it and it was something that would make a difference to people's safety on board ships.

Being involved in providing this security was the type of thing that was becoming more and more important to me - making a difference for people.

This other lad and I knew each other, but not well. He was self-employed too and had the same mindset as I had.

When something was working out and paying off for me, I enjoyed it so much that I would look for the next opportunity to move on. Any money the company made I would just reinvest straight back into the company to allow me to travel or to purchase what was needed for the next part of my plan.

I had kept the fact I had MS to myself, because at this stage the other two in the team didn't need to know, but it was my plan to tell them further down the line after I had proved my worth.

The meeting was over two days, and it was largely about getting to know each other. The other two men had done a fair bit of work together so it was more about them getting to know me, my past experience and my thoughts on the plan.

Now, back to health - and unfortunately I need to mention urine again. It was always a worry back then while I was still adjusting to things. When going into this type of situation where I didn't know my surroundings, I would rig myself up to a tube and put a leg bag on. This would allow me to relax and not panic if I unexpectedly needed to visit the toilet in a rush. This leg bag allowed me to act normally when needed. Leg bags also allowed me to travel for long distances in cars or trains and relax. It was another one of my medical friends.

So here we were in the car heading down south for this meeting. I had my bag on the inner side of my left calf, hidden under my trouser leg. The plan was for me to empty it at service stations along the way, just like a normal pee stop. It was all fitting in perfectly.

Perfectly, that is, until the other lad decided we would be best to just head straight for the hotel as the traffic was moving nicely for a Friday afternoon. I quietly agreed, because it did make sense to stay on the road and head straight there, in one long run. He had done his maths and decided he had enough fuel. I was not too concerned about this. I had my back up bag in place. What I didn't know, and was about to find out, was that the bag was leaking when under pressure.

The trip seemed to be going on and on and my bag became under more and more pressure. My heart sank when I felt wet-ness. The bag had given. It was awful; I had just wet myself in his car. What was I going to do? I had to tell him about this very embarrassing situation. I had just wet myself sitting next to him. Anyway, details are not required. It led to me coming clean (not quite the correct wording here, I know). I told of my situation. I also told how it would not affect my ability to get involved with the plan. The security required was all in my head. I pushed the point that if anything my 'Mega Stubborn' approach to life was a good thing in business.

He was very understanding although shocked with this news. We pulled over at the next petrol station and I went and got changed, another of my many embarrassing walks to the toilet over the years.

As you can imagine, over the next couple of days the conversation made its way back to my health on a number of occasions, but we got to the meeting and it all went ahead as planned. After the two days of being down there talking about our plan we finished up, said our goodbyes and all headed home.

I was excited about this. It was a taste of my old life in the Marines and business mixed together, proper excitement and a dream come true! I finally made it home with a lot of thoughts about logistics, security teams and new opportunities going round in my head.

Back home I went walking on the Innellan road thinking deeply about the plan, while cracking the usual three mile walk that's so familiar to me. On this particular day I decided to phone the other two for a catch-up on things. They wouldn't answer the phone. I tried time and time again but they wouldn't answer. What was going on? They didn't reply to my emails, my texts or my phone calls. It quickly became apparent they had ditched me from the team. They didn't want me on it any more.

This situation cut me very deep. I was having such positive

thoughts on life again, the plan was going to be so good for me, and also making the kind of little change to the world that I had been wanting to make. Admittedly, though, I was still relatively new to business and being hurt by this was a touch naïve. I was still not earning any money with my business back in the Clyde. Like I said earlier, any profit made went straight back into the company to push it forward.

A key point was that I now had such energy and excitement with this opportunity that I could not just switch it off. I had just been ditched and didn't think I should have been. The reason they had ditched me was not a concern to me, and I know what I was capable of.

I had been through a lot by then, and my view in life had changed, but to be honest, I viewed my experiences as valuable ones. Yes, I wanted to make life comfortable and financially secure for Zander and our family. I had started to appreciate things in life that until now I had taken for granted, things I had experienced every day but had never given them the energy and respect they were worthy of. I would say this was because I had been fortunate enough to have them while growing up - a car, petrol for the car, heating in the house, a house, clean water coming out the taps in the house, a doctor and a chemist to visit after seeing the doctor.

Other than taking enough from the company's success to give comfort and security to the family, I wanted to somehow make a difference. I wanted to help areas of the world that were financially poor such as Somalia. The company's product was designed to be used for non-lethal security in the trouble spots of the world. More often than not these areas were financially broke, third world countries.

When you have been so low and received unsettling news such as "you have Multiple Sclerosis", and the following day you are waiting to find out if you are going to die, I can assure you, your views change!

The way I am considering it, I have been fortunate enough to view what the end of life feels like. I've then been handed it back. I was not about to sit and let life pass me by any more. Yes, I have been a guy who has tried and failed, but more importantly I've been a guy who has tried and succeeded. I will continue to try. I know I will occasionally fail but more importantly, and the bit I care about and focus on, is the belief that I will succeed too. Is that not what it's all about? Realisation and experience.

It's been something I could only start to realise gradually over time; years, actually. My situation had come round because of having MS. You see, over time I started to consider MS my friend. Yes, my friend. I had it, so get on with it. Yes, it is tough but I was starting to realise it was also the reason for so much joy.

Chapter 32 – A Beautiful Mind And A Beautiful Boy

Zander was now one year old. He had started walking at ten months. No, that's not quite true. He had started running at ten months. Ever since he was born, the part-time risk assessor in me has been promoted and given a full-time place. It was now more important than it had ever been before. But I was delighted with this. There was nothing this wee guy could do that was wrong in my book. Yes, he would push the boundaries, and yes, he would be in trouble with his parents for it. Deep down though, I was enjoying watching his antics; it was something that gave me such pleasure and also an almighty kick in the backside regarding my endurance and physical ability. How could I let my physical failings affect my ability to be Zander's father?

My health was changing. I was now two years into living with this condition, but it was still tough to get used to not having my usual physicality. I had lived my life using my physical ability to its highest level and was now having to use catheters to go for a pee.

I had also noticed my views changing about everyday life. I was seeing through a parent's eyes. Until then, if I had heard a young child cry I would wish it would just hurry up and stop. But when Zander cried, whether in the middle of the night or during the day, Sarah or I would go to him straight away to make sure that he was OK. It was nothing to do with the noise.

Stopping him crying was all about making him comfy; it was all about him. He was our inspiration for keeping ourselves secure and well.

I was pushing business hard – and what a learning curve that was. I was studying other companies, what they did, how they did it, and wondering if I could I do it where we lived. Looking back, it's clear to see that I was subconsciously moulding my life to be the way I wanted it to be and, as far as I was concerned, how it needed it to be in those days. The human mind is far more powerful than people realise - but more on that later.

I'd had the horrendous flare up some two years before, and that was my lowest point. Until I started to write this book, that was a time in life that I had not allowed myself to revisit. I didn't let my mind go there. I had read self-help books, eaten specific diets; I was visiting the hyperbaric chamber weekly for oxygen. I had been on detox retreats and I was managing my stress through running and pushing on my own business forward.

I must admit, though, that while I wouldn't dwell on my first MS attack, I knew the signs. I had been down that road before and I knew it went to a place that was hideous. It was not a place I wanted to go ever again. But I had been the son back then. I had the unquestioning love and support of my parents and Sarah throughout that time. Life was now different. I was the dad. It was my time to show the son what life was about. Making Zander look up to me was now paramount in my life.

Leading the way through the start of his life was my place, and a greatly valued role. Yes I do live in fear of the unmentionable coming back and yes it does terrify me. But the enjoyment and love I have for life is now far greater than the fear, so enjoyment is easier to focus on. I have learned what doesn't help me and what makes life nasty again. A hangover, for example, mentally brings me down to a place I don't like and make me look in the wrong direction, so don't really drink much these days.

I had been released from hospital around two years before, but my health was a daily reality. I would have a good day, then a hard day. It was quite normal to have the occasional good week, then a bad week. I didn't seem to notice when I was having a good time, but I certainly noticed when I was ghastly. It's strange how you naturally notice feeling poorly, but you don't notice when you're feeling well.

Anyway, since my initial flare up I have always had numb sensations that rush through my body. On some days, I would have obvious restricted physical ability. I would say it was similar to the character in the movie 'A Beautiful Mind'. Russell Crowe plays the part of a schizophrenic genius trying to carry on with his life while ignoring all the make-believe people in his mind.

MS is always there, but in the back ground. I could feel it. I chose to ignore it; it was 'only that background noise again' that I deliberately chose not to hear. I'm sure that if I were to stop and talk to it, then it would happily spark up a conversation with me and hang around a while. But on the days that it would try to hold me back in bed, or say to me: 'Don't bother going for your walk today, it's raining', I would make a point of getting out my Gore-Tex and walking - or should I say dragging my foot - a bit further than the day before. This is no exaggeration; I'm talking about a limp that might make cars pull over to check that everything was OK. In my determination to make progress every single day, I would refuse all offers of a lift.

By this point I had already started to tell people that I was doing the Three Peaks mountain challenge the following year. I had set a date, so training was on my mind. Success at the end of Ben Nevis, and ultimately being a normal father to Zander, was what was dominated my thoughts. I was focusing on meeting that mountain challenge.

I pushed the physical struggle daily so that it just became my normality. Yeah, it was hard, but it was just life. If you can accept the situation and the discomfort and hardship, you can make it normal and avoid focusing on it; that's how I viewed it then and this is how I view it now. The Marine in me again?

Chapter 33 – Another Coincidence?

I believe coincidences are all around us. Well, actually, if I'm going to be honest I don't consider them coincidences at all; I don't actually believe coincidences exist. In life you have to believe in something; ask for it, and then believe it will happen. Let me give you an example of this.

I had visited the hyperbaric chamber at the PDA one particular morning. I had now made the chamber a weekly visit to keep my body rich in oxygen and my tissues saturated. There isn't too much to do in the chamber other than breathe in pure oxygen and think about things for an hour at a time.

Over the past while I had been having thoughts about how this was actually working and helping keep my body good. Do I really need to keep coming in here? This was a good while after my initial flare up. I was working hard at the marina and in a routine. Time in the chamber was a good time for thinking and planning. I now knew when to say yes, and when to say no at work too.

So, I had been in the chamber and was walking from the Professional Dive Academy (PDA) to my office, which is only 1 kilometre away. With my body saturated in oxygen and the Marina being so close, walking to work just made sense.

I was on a good day, my energy was good, but I knew I would be tired in the afternoon; I always was on chamber days. I went into the office and went through my usual routine of starting up my laptop and making a coffee.

About half an hour later an older gentleman walked in and asked to speak with Paul Kerr. He was smart but casually dressed and exceptionally polite. He introduced himself as Charles Gillies. I immediately thought I should take this Charles Gillies into the coffee shop next door for a real coffee and talk with him there.

Charles told me he had a yacht called Spring Cloud in the marina and wondered if I would sit next to him while he did some close quarter marina manoeuvres. He told me he was relatively new to sailing but thoroughly enjoyed it.

The two of us walked down to the berth Spring Cloud was on. The yacht was an older 17-foot Corby. I don't know too much about sailing, but it was only the 'bringing it alongside' he was interested in. We decided to have lunch together and then go out in it afterwards.

Over lunch it became clear to me that Charles was a very well-to-do individual. When he spoke you couldn't help but give him 110 per cent of your attention. He had totally won over my respect from the off with how he conducted himself. But the thing that really got me was, the feeling seemed to be mutual and that he also had respect for me. Yet he didn't even know me! Meeting Charles Gillies that day was a great experience in itself, like a privilege, or, something, but I didn't quite know why.

We went down to Spring Cloud and I went through my usual questions. We covered the pre-start engine checks, safety questions and a few other checks. Charles was a brilliant student. Once we were both happy with what we had discussed and were about to head out on the water, we fired the engine up, cast off the lines and headed out of the marina. Charles would be at the helm steering the boat, and I was going to act as his crew.

Once out of the marina we turned the boat in the middle of the Holy Loch and started to head back in as if we had been out all day and this was us now returning home. As crew I advised Charles that I was going to prep the bow and stern lines ready for tying the boat up when coming alongside the pontoon. I came back and sat next to Charles at the helm again.

Our next discussion blew my mind; honestly, it blew my mind! It changed my views on everything and what I had previously thought about life and the questions you ask yourself.

"Paul, I hope you don't mind me saying but you look slightly unsteady on your feet", Charles said. I thought: "Well the cat's out the bag now", so I just told Charles about the morning's activity. I told him that I had Multiple Sclerosis and had been in the hyperbaric chamber earlier. "The hyperbaric chamber always makes me tired in the afternoon", I added.

Charles' next comment was one that I will remember for the rest of my life. Remember, this polite and impressive gentleman had randomly walked into my office in the Holy Loch Marina that very morning after I had been in the hyperbaric chamber and he had been looking for my help.

"Paul, I'm Professor Charles Gillies. I've been involved in the research of hyperbaric therapy in different illnesses, one being MS, so I know a good bit about this subject."

So here I was in the company of this distinguished gentleman, who was an expert in the very field that was closest to me at that moment. I was able to question him closely about various aspects of my condition and its treatment in the hyperbaric chamber. He had just dropped into my life exactly when I needed answers.

This is another area I'm finding hard to put into words. I have come to believe, from the experiences which I've had over the years, that there has to be more to it. Sometimes you just say to yourself: "What a coincidence, I can't believe that just happened, must be fate."

Well I believe this can happen to everyone, if you ask for it. I mentioned previously that your 'thoughts fuel fires'. Looking back over history, every single thing that has been created by man, everything that has been built, everything that has been invented, all began with a single thought from a single person.

Today's world has made it common to focus on what we can't do, what we can't have, how difficult life is and how the path life will take is going to be a tough one.

I believe that if you think like that and you believe that, then the world will give you what you're thinking.

This is due to the same line of thought of the great inventors I mentioned earlier; John Logie Baird for example. He 'thought' about inventing the television and he did. Henry Ford 'thought' about the car, and the list goes on.

At the time everyone thought these guys were mental. All I'm commenting on is my thoughts and the facts I have kept my focused on over the years to help myself. I don't mean this to sound rude but whether you agree with me or not is irrelevant to me. I have learned that it's my thoughts that matter to me. Yes a doctor can tell me what is wrong with me, but from that point on, I am the one who will decide what's going to happen.

I started to climb the hill, so I'll finish climbing the hill!

Chapter 34 – Lamp Post To Lamp Post

I had been to work one particular day and I was home early. It was a lovely evening. I have never been one to stay in the house when the weather is good and I had started walking every day, not to pass time but purposely to push myself physically to the stage of being unable to go any further.

I'd leave the house and walk down Wellington Street and on to the shore road that goes alongside the River Clyde to Innellan, where my parents live. The Bullwood Quarry is only one and a half miles along this coast road from Maymor. Mentally, I was back at my parents' hallway with my Royal Marines Fartlek training tactic. But this time, I was not using the small black tiles on the floor as my distance markers; I had progressed steadily to Fartleking between lamp posts. I was also using them as a way to push out my distance further, lamp post by lamp post, and day by day. If I felt like it, I would go one lamp post further than I had the day before. It was usually around about the Bullwood Quarry when I turned around and was then back on the home straight.

I had saved the most motivating iPod tunes for this. Occasionally, my iPod would run out of charge. When this happened, it was as if my world had collapsed. If I didn't have the rock legend Dave Grohl pushing me down the Innellan road with his Monkey Wrench, the effort was so much harder. But you know me – I always cracked on until I made it home.

I remember one day meeting Carol and Martin at the top of Wellington Street while returning from my three-mile round trip quarry walk. Going back up Wellington Street was like scaling Mount Everest. No dramas though; I have always wanted to climb Mount Everest! I always looked forward to this point of the walk as it was somewhere I targeted as a marker. It required me to take five at the bottom of the hill to get my act together before stepping up my momentum. By this point in the walk regardless of it being a good day or bad, I always felt like breeze blocks had been sneakily tied to each arm and ankle.

I was limping badly, and my energy was at a low-day level. Carol and Martin were managers in the parent company that had owned ProAdventure. We stopped at the corner of Wellington Street and had a quick catch up. Man, I was tired by this point. I could tell that they were shocked to see what was standing in front of them.

The last time they had seen me I was a young fit former Royal Marine. The way I was struggling and just standing there is still very clear in my mind. I had to hold onto a garden hedge to keep myself steady, while my legs were actually shaking. Carol at one point put her hand out to stop me; she thought I was falling over. I was used to people reacting like that.

Something became very clear to me that day. I knew every day that I had to lift my training because I knew I would get to the top of these three peaks that were challenging me to come forward. Any time that I felt as if I could go further, then that's what I did - I stepped out harder and reached yet another lamp post.

Every day I was experiencing a drastic problem with my training, and this was something that willpower or ignoring made no difference to. It's a perfect example of what living with MS is like. Some days my limp would be worse than others. On my best days, I could walk two miles before the limping started. On my worst days, I wondered how I had walked two miles the day before. On the good days, I would start my walks rather sprightly, looking like a normal healthy guy.

These days were great. The old favourites like the Foo Fighters instantly got me into my stride. Walks were good for my thinking too. If I had a problem with work or if an area of what I was doing required some thought, I could think about these things while I walked. Keeping my brain active stopped me from focusing on trivial health problem that might only ever happen on that one day.

I have said it before and I'm saying it again - thoughts fuel fires, good and bad, so think about what you're thinking - keep your thoughts worthy of your time and always productive. I can't stress enough the importance of this!

What was unfolding at the same time, and the most active part of my motivation, was Zander's development. He was pushing his training too. His walking and running were rapid, and though for now I was able to keep up with him, his energy was fabulous. He was certainly getting close to overtaking me with his speed and endurance.

I was strict with him, far more so than other parents, but I had my reasons. The way I saw it was that if I told him not to do something, then I had to be sure that he wasn't going to do it. I've put myself through such anxiety about this. I was terrified that he would go to do something dangerous and I couldn't get myself to him quickly enough to stop him. I worried about whether he might step on to a dangerous road, or drink or swallow something that he shouldn't. If I shouted to him to stop, I had to be certain that this was what he would do.

I didn't have to worry when Zander was with Sarah, as she is such a good mother and she had these areas covered. I had adopted the old-fashioned style of parenting, the kind I had from my parents. I managed to make it known to Zander that he was the most important thing in my life. But I had also managed to make him know that it's 'Do as I say - when I say'.

A very recent example of these tactics was when he had been in trouble at school while in Primary One. Sarah and I went up to the school with Zander and asked him to explain to us, in front of the teacher, in her office, what he had done wrong. He was then asked to apologise to the teacher, there and then, in front of us.

After school, when we were in the supermarket I told Zander to carry a shopping basket instead of me pushing a shopping trolley. I explained to him that I was still cross with him about school and that he was going to carry the basket until we reached the checkout.

I walked quickly, filling up the basket that he was carrying. He was finding it tough but he was managing it. He was out of breath, and was getting tired, but he kept up with me. After this, I said very seriously: "Well done for keeping up with me there Zander, I'm proud of you for doing that." We high-fived and I explained to him that this was his punishment for mis-behaving in school that day. And whether we talked about it again would be up to him, but I would not be bringing it up again. For me it was over; I wanted it to be over for him too. Our relationship was so strong that Zander and I both knew that this incident was one to learn from, but not one to repeat.

Chapter 35 – A Red Herring

I had been experiencing problems with my left eye in late September 2007 when blank spots appeared in its centre. At the start, it was like a 'blind dot' floating around and was very disorienting. My eye was also very painful. It alternated between feeling as if it was about to explode, and then every so often, it was as if someone had jabbed a red hot needle into it.

Over a matter of only a few days I became completely blind in my left eye. I had lost eyesight before, but not like this. This was happening while I was experiencing some of the most horrendous pain you could imagine. Again Glen, my GP, was my rescuer.

As soon as I saw him he immediately made all the phone calls necessary to bring in the consultant neurologist and ophthalmologist. I couldn't have been treated better.

The last time I had been in to see Glen was four months earlier when I had been given a drug to try. It was a weekly injection that I had to give myself through a small hand-held machine. It was a deep intramuscular injection and, if I'm honest, it was quite traumatic.

After the injection I would instantly bleed quite heavily from the injection site. Writing this is making my laugh – and cringe. The needle was maybe two and a half inches long. While I was pressing a button the needle went plunging straight down and into my leg, all two and a half inches of it. I then pushed the injector and the medicine went in. The machine shone a wee torch onto my leg with a target on it like a rifle sight. But for some reason, I was bleeding quite badly after it and this was happening week after week. I eventually took a close look at the needle and noticed that the end was bent around and had made itself into something like a very small fish hook.

I took it to Glen the next day to let him see it. It was decided that the needle was too long for my muscle size. It was blunting itself on my thigh bone when it went into the muscle. It was tough to get it back out from deep within the muscle, I can assure you. Oddly enough there was no sensation or pain from this. It sounds weird and unimaginable, but none of this hurt me, my legs are always numb. What luck! Shorter needles were ordered - problem solved.

Anyway, to get to the blindness in my left eye. This was classed as another MS flare up, but I was more relaxed about it because I was told that, in time, my vision would more than likely return. About three days later, I received a letter asking me to go up to the Southern General for a consultation. Let me stress something - you don't just get a letter asking you to come up to Neurology in two days unless it's vital. So Sarah, Zander, and 'eye' went back to see what was up.

It's weird how well you adapt to knowing your way around a department as important as Neurology. I knew where I was going, I knew there was nothing awful for Z to see, otherwise he wouldn't have been there. It was a simple ground-floor walk, straight into a routine check-up and a chat with the neurologist; that's all I expected to happen.

The neurologist talked about a number of different medications. He mentioned one in particular that really stood out. The way I saw this was that I had a serious problem and surely a serious problem required serious actions. The neurologist mentioned a chemotherapy drug that is used for MS. This jumped out at me. There was to be a two-year chemo plan. It would be given every three months.

The consultant said: "After the two years of chemo you will go on to a daily injection, but not like the one you're on now, but a very fine needle that's about 8mm long, like a diabetic uses. You can adjust the depth of the penetration of this kind of needle."

I had a lot of questions, as you can imagine. Will it make me infertile – possibly. Will my hair fall out – possibly. Will it make me sick at all - yes, certainly! And on, and on.

The main questions to ask were how it works and how effective it is. As I have mentioned, MS is the immune system attacking the nervous system. The chemotherapy was to shut down my immune system and then when it came back on, this chemo drug would have 'retuned' it to be my 'friend'. It was to have good outcomes for me. After the two years, the injection was to act like a red herring to my system. If the immune system was still looking to attack something, injecting the 'Copaxon' daily would give it something else to attack instead.

Sarah and I had stuff to think about and discuss. In her usual fashion she was a rock. That's all I can say of her, my rock. My urine and body fluids would become toxic for the week following my chemo. There was a chance that I would become infertile. Sure, we had Zander, but having him highlighted the importance of this chemo option, despite any possible negative sides.

What about having toxic bodily fluids with a youngster around the house? We were given a document to take away with us on how to manage this. Always sit down on the toilet. Flush a few times after use, and so on. Wash your towel straight away after a shower. No hot tubs and so on. In the end it was a family decision that the chemo was too good an opportunity to miss. Everything added up and the way it worked made total sense to us all. Yeah, there were potential downsides to it, which could be pretty brutal, but the pros were too good to ignore. So, I made a visit back to Glen to get the ball rolling and, as always, he did everything very promptly.

I was called back to the Southern General. I required more blood tests, an electrocardiogram (ECG); I had to freeze sperm too. This was a tall order! I'd never had to produce to order like this before and especially with my whole family knowing about it too.

Chapter 36 – "Don't Be Shy"

A couple of weeks had passed and I was I was to start my first course of chemotherapy. I was to go up to the hospital that day and I was feeling excited but also scared. I knew this was possibly the start of a big improvement in my health. But I also knew that I was in for a rough week once I had been given this drug. Was it going to make me infertile? How ill was I going to be this week? What about Zander? Was my toxic pee, sweat, or saliva going to be a problem to him? I couldn't kiss my one-year-old son for a week.

Anyway, as I was thinking about the journey the phone rang. Sarah called me through, saying it was my neurologist at the Southern General. My first thoughts were: the neurologist has called me at home on the morning of the day I was to start my chemo? Why? I carried the phone through to our bedroom, closed the door and sat on our bed. A strange conversation unfolded.

"Paul, your bloods from your last checks have come back. We have found a problem with your liver. You can't start your chemo until we have found out what this is."

Of course, I was disappointed about this. I wanted this medication that I had already decided was going to change my life. I felt I should carry on the conversation politely. Not to sound, well, disappointed I suppose, but to question the plan moving forward.

"What do you think it is, doctor?"

"At this point, we have no idea."

By now, I knew not to beat about the bush. I also knew how to make this known to the doctors in a way that relaxed them about having to break bad news to me.

"Could it be cancer?"

"I don't know."

So, the conversation ended and I changed my day's plan. I was now going back to work to crack on with my normal day. I was not starting my chemo today - because I might have cancer? It was strange. Did I now have cancer as well as my MS? But isn't chemo for cancer?

That same afternoon my mobile rang when I was down at my company's RIB, the boat 'P2'. The call was from my neurologist, and as he had already arranged it with my doctor, he asked me to pop into the GP for him to take more bloods. He also said that from the papers he now had in front of him it was very unlikely to be cancer. In fact, it was very unlikely to be a big deal at all. So I went to see Glen and had my blood taken again.

It turned out all was well and my first day of chemo was booked again for the following week.

As usual Sarah stepped up to the mark. She drove me to the Southern General and came in with me. Zander was at Sarah's dad Duncan's that day. I walked into the all-too-familiar Neurology department and was back up at the fourth floor. It was once a scary floor, and this was the reason why Zander was not with us that day. This time, I was a lad with experience.

But I was also a lad with a plan, a lad with a vision. I had experience from a very low place, and I had a plan to get back to places that were unimaginably high for me these days.

These were the highest mountains in Wales, England and Scotland, and they were to be climbed in only eight months' time. This chemo was going to help me. I had already decided this. I'm going to say that again: I had decided that this chemo was going to help me. I had decided that I would be better than I was.

I had to give a urine test to make sure I didn't have a bladder infection, and then they brought out the drug for my first dose of chemotherapy. It was a clear bag of electric blue fluid. They rigged it up into a complex tube system. It was to be administered in conjunction with a couple of other bags. This process watered down the intensity of the drug in my system. Apparently it would have been too intense for my liver to deal with otherwise. This all made sense. That is why they had focused so much on my liver's behaviour and had insisted that everything must be perfect with it beforehand. Once all rigged up they inserted the intravenous needle into my arm and started to drip in the electric blue fluid.

The next strange part of my life began. Here I was, getting my first of eight doses of chemotherapy, and this was to turn my immune system off! The part of my body that was meant to protect me from illness had to be turned off purposely, as it was destroying me. Isn't the human body weird?

I had also been having problems peeing. It's about the most natural thing in the world to do, as well as being one of the first things in the world you learn to do! It's just having a pee! Well, not any more. To a normal healthy person it is very simple. To someone with MS it was becoming a total epic.

I seemed to be always bursting but never able to go. After having a pee that seemed to have taken forever, sometimes taking 30 minutes and coming out like a Morse code message, I immediately needed to go again straight away. But even when planned, and in a toilet, I couldn't seem to urinate, I would eventually leave the toilet still bursting but unable to go.

Ok, let's take a step away quickly. I can best describe a bladder as being like a balloon. It fills up gradually, but when required it comes under pressure to empty.

Believe it or not, your bladder is a sterile container that means it's free from bacteria. It's only once your urine has left your body that it becomes dirty and starts to gather bacteria. If you get a bacterial infection in your bladder, it's a tough one for your body to manage. These infections are generally relatively easy to get rid of, but it messes with your body whilst there.

So, my most recent MS problems were with the wee sphincters in my urethra that tell your brain when they're under pressure and there's a need to visit the toilet. They weren't listening to me. When my brain was telling my body: 'Ok, that's us at the toilet now, you can relax and have a pee', my body was not hearing the message. Although I might feel as if I was bursting, no pee would emerge. I was walking around with a bladder full of urine that would only give a little release of pressure when I was absolutely bursting, and it would only get just past the bursting stage, but it would never empty.

Just to ramp up this new excitement, as soon as I got into a position of not being allowed to pee, I would suddenly and uncontrollably start to do one, and it would happen in all kinds of situations.

For example on the RIB P2 with people who had possibly hired me to spread the ashes of a family member; on the bus; in the car on the motorway; or visiting church (a new-found pastime).

So life became very unpredictable. To add to this, I was also starting to have bladder complications, as walking around with a bladder full of 'stale' urine is not good for you.

By the time I was on chemotherapy, my immune system was very low (this was all part of the chemo plan though). Chemo was harsh on my bladder and was making me wet the bed regularly, along with my now poisonous body fluid. I had a bladder full of stale pee and no immune system to combat infection.

So I booked into see Glen to discuss what could be done and, yet again, I needed to go to a hospital across the water for a consultation with a urologist. The urologist tried to put me at ease and said: "Don't worry; I do this 50 times a day". Little did I know it, but my Marines' background and experience of often being seen naked was about to come into play yet again.

Her opening comment just made me laugh: "OK Paul, drop your trousers and underpants. Don't be shy, I have seen every type of knob you could ever imagine, big, small, squint - you name it, I will have seen it so don't worry about it!"

While she was talking to me she had very noticeably, and very worryingly, just pulled a 12-inch thin plastic tube from a box. It was in a wrapper which had a wee built-in bag of lubricant in it.

As I was standing there in front of this lady, with my trousers and my boxers at my ankles, I was wondering what she was about to ask me to do with this 12-inch lubricated tube.

My willy had shrivelled up as tight and shy as I had ever experienced before. I had been under the spell of 'the wee head rules the big head' many times before, but this was very different.

She handed the tube to me, which in mind was getting longer and fatter the more I looked at it. She discussed the importance of personal hygiene and that I must not touch the tip of the tube with my hands. Why was she telling me this?

She then advised me to start sticking the 12 inch tube into my willy until urine started to come out!

My reply was very simple. I started to laugh nervously and said: "Are you mental?"

In no uncertain terms she told me to get on with it.

So I started to feed this 12-inch pipe into my pee hole. I got to a stage where it was probably 8 inches into me, and if it had made a noise, it would have been a high-pitched nervous squealing deep inside my lower stomach.

At this point, the fact that I was almost naked and doing this very personal deed in front of this lady in Glasgow, was irrelevant. I was in Glasgow, far from home, and this was simply her job. What she said next was hilarious though and made me laugh aloud; it really did break the ice: "You're from Dunoon are you not, Paul? Do you not work at the Marina?"

The joke was that the answer to all her questions was my wide-eyed nodding in agreement!

Anyway, I hadn't realised the discomfort that I had been in over these past few months. That day of sticking the 12-inch tube into my willy made my life so much better. I could go back to bed, not bursting for the toilet and I would no longer wet the bed once I was asleep. I wasn't carrying stale urine around all day in my bladder that was messing up my body's functioning even more. I was no longer wetting myself when getting into the car, and so on, and so on.

Yeah I had to use catheters, but they quickly became my normality and my new best friend. I loved them. It's a bit like toothache. No-one enjoys going to the dentist. But when you have wild tooth ache, you can't wait for the jab and for the dentist to start the drilling.

Chapter 37 – Reflecting The New Me

I briefly mentioned my Wrangler Jeep earlier; it was a summer car that I would drive on good days and that I would put away on wet days. I had bought it when I had just started at ProAdventure at a time in life when I didn't really have any responsibilities or worries. I had come back from four months working out of South Georgia. I was paid well there and had nowhere to splash my cash.

When I had been very young I had this very impressive toy Wrangler Jeep called a Penny Spinner. My Gran had bought me it in Oxfam one day as a wee treat. It was one of those toys that you could not put a value on. It was fast, did stunts and fitted in my pocket. You could put a one pence piece in the back of it, wind it up on the floor, and it would drive off very quickly doing crazy wheelies and great tricks around the kitchen. I loved it! Due to this wee Oxfam present I had grown up liking the real version of Wrangler Jeeps.

So, there I was working in ProAdventure, loving windsurfing, mountain biking, and generally my usual active outdoor world. Driving into the ProAdventure office one summer's day I saw sitting, at the side of the road with a 'for sale' sign on it, a red Wrangler Jeep.

You know that way, when your actions go forward on their own somehow, and you just sit at the side and let them? I pulled into the place where it was parked and had a look around it. My next action was to get back into my company L200 and get Mitch from the office to hear his thoughts about the possible purchase of this ludicrous car. I bought it that night!

This completely impractical, expensive to run, rugged yet robust, and dependable car was a must. It was effectively like looking in the mirror and seeing a Jeep staring back at me. I loved it from the off. You wouldn't think it though. It was thrown in at the deep end getting stuck in rivers, fields, up mountains.

On the days the weather permitted taking it to work it must have got nervous seeing the sun coming up.

Like Kyle our pup though, this part of my life had to take a back seat when things changed. It was pushed to the side and uncaringly parked up at my parent's house in the drive. As far out of the way as possible, it became background scenery. It was left as far in the corner of my parents' drive as possible, and forgotten about.

I was out walking and visiting my parents one day about a month before The Three Peaks Challenge. It was a good way to get training in - and some food at the end of it. I had walked the three miles out to their house from Maymor. It was July. I was having my own secret thoughts about whether I was going to live up to the challenge.

The usual concerns - what if I have flare up just before it? I had already raised a good sum of money for charity, how would I give it all back? I had been training hard, climbing a good number of mountains with Brendon, going up the 'Camel's Hump' hill behind Dunoon in the evenings, and doing the quarry walk every night too. If I had climbed a hill that day with Brendon then I would be sure to do the quarry walk as well. Yes it was tough, but it was also a way to shake the lactic acid out my legs. I considered this second walk of the day a vital one. In the end I was about to crack three mountains in 24 hours, so this was a realistic requirement for me.

So, I had walked out to my parent's house one sunny Sunday, about a month before the 1st of August, the day the Three Peaks was arranged to take place. Mum and Dad have quite a steep drive and by the time I got to the house I had my usual 'car stopping' limp. I literally dragged myself up the drive and took a seat on the small wall next to where the Jeep was carefully abandoned.

I sat there for my usual five minute recharge; the usual time it takes before cracking on. But my focus was now on my Jeep and how sorry it was looking. I had never really noticed it. I had been so focused on myself this past while. The car I once considered to be me was still very much me. It was sitting side on to the hill. The two lower tyres had deflated and it was lying quite dramatically to the side. It had been sitting there for three years and it was covered in moss and leaves.

I remembered Dad had told me he had drained the radiator fluid to avoid it freezing and cracking during the winter; and he had also removed the battery. I opened the door and had a look inside it. It had water up to the sills and was covered in mould. What a state! It was heart-breaking to see. I sat back down on the wall next to it. I was sad at this. This Jeep which had been a reflection of the old me, was now certainly reflecting the new me.

PK, the sun is out and you have some time and energy, why not put some time into it? I needed Euan my brother-in-law again, and Richie my closest mate who owns Cowal Car Components.

I made some phone calls to them, and sourced a foot pump, a jerry can, some anti-freeze, oil and a charged battery. I took Mum's car and drove round getting everything I needed and then made my way back to Goldenlea to start getting it all sorted.

The 4x4 tyres are hard ones to pump up when you have MS I can tell you. I had to adopt the 'doing some exercise' approach; it was more than just pumping up tyres. I filled the radiator with anti-freeze, and added 10 litres of petrol. I dipped the engine for oil. I was amazed at how golden looking the oil inside the engine was. It was at the perfect level and very clean looking.

I cut the top off a milk carton and took out a sponge from Mum and Dad's bathroom. I emptied the water out of the sills which had seeped in over the past three years. I fitted the battery and climbed into the driver's seat. I turned the key one click. I was met again by my old friend Dave Grohl from the Foo fighters. In shocked panic at this loud music I turned the stereo down while at the same time being very pleased that at least that was still working. At that point Dad walked up to me, sitting in the Jeep laughing and said: "What are you doing Paul? It's been three years. It's not been moved." But in true Dad fashion he couldn't help but pull up his sleeves and get involved with this.

If it was going to run, then I had to start somewhere; at least this was a beginning to it moving again. I turned the key and the starter motor turned; it sounded strong. It turned over maybe eight times and to our total amazement it fired up. I was in stunned, delighted, and emotional silence. This Jeep which had mirrored me at my strongest had stayed there, and then mirrored me at my weakest. And now, just before the Three Peaks Challenge when I was having inward reservations about it, my Jeep showed me that it was still strong and was ready for my next command. I was going to succeed with the Three Peaks. That was decided that day, there and then. I had no more worries about this.

The Jeep

Chapter 38 – Zander's First Bike

Zander was nearly two years old. On one particular day we were both down town on Dunoon's Argyll Street. It was a lovely day, the sun was out and the street was busy like it always is on a sunny Saturday. We were slowly making our way up Argyll Street when we were met by an energetic young girl on a 'new to me style' type of bike. It was made of wood! It had no pedals and was pushed along by the kid's feet; but it had proper bike steering and wheels and moved very well. It was great and Zander loved it; something this father immediately noticed. The girl turned from where we were standing and went up to her mum.

It was Helen, an old friend of my sister Nicola. I had known her since I was Zander's age but had not seen her for many years, as she had moved up to Glasgow to go to college and I had gone to the Marines.

Anyway, this was Katie, Helen's daughter. Helen and I had a quick catch up of the past ten years while Zander looked at Katie's bike with total confusion and envy. While Helen and I were talking, Katie went flying off up the street again. I liked the way this balance bike was designed, not just physically but also the idea as a whole. A real bike made of wood, pushed by her feet, with no pedals to get in the way.

I wanted my 18-month-old son on one of these bikes as soon as

I could get my hands on one. Once home, I immediately opened Google and entered the details I had been given by Helen on this 'balance bike'. Zander had learned from Katie that it was called Joey and he made this very clear to me while looking for it online. It seemed to address all the balance problems kids have while learning to ride a bike. I could get Z on this, and then by the time he was big enough to get on the smallest pedal bike I could find, he would already have the balance part of it naturally squared away.

It was becoming obvious to me that Zander was a very energetic, capable young boy. I was noticing this in the strangest way, because I was finding it harder to match his pace while watching over him. He was becoming faster and more physically able in life. I am going to try and write this so you see how I was at the same time concerned, yet delighted.

I was once this young fit lad who was lucky enough to have experienced a good bit of life's physical joys. I now had a one-and-a half year old son who was following in my footsteps; it was all go for Z. I couldn't wish for him to be anything other than he was.

As I was seeing him slowly progressing, the 'background noise' was slowly getting noisy again. Not from a health point of view, but from a proud father's viewpoint. I knew from how I felt, and what my body was telling me, that Zander was starting to require more of what energy I had. Did I have much more in me though? It was always something I was delighted to give him regardless, of how it made me feel; but it was getting to the stage where I soon wouldn't be able to keep up with him, and the thought of this possibility broke my heart.

How can I do this father/son role? How will I keep up with him and at the same time lead him? As far as I was concerned, this was so important to him. Me. Us! I wanted it to be in a capable, influential and impressive way. The way I had learned from my father.

Chapter 39 – Things Change

Over those two and a half years of clawing back some physical ability, I had been experimenting with everything from my old life that I knew I could do back then. I wanted to know where my ability now stood having this long-term health issue. I wanted to know every area of what I could now do. I've tried it all, from badminton to roller skating. I will let you decide for yourself how those particular experiments went!

Thanks for lending me the roller skates Richie, and thanks for the bandages afterwards Claire.

Even though my walking could quickly become a visible struggle, sometimes even over short distances, I had discovered I could ride a bike with ease and continue this over distance - you can't see a limp while riding a bike. No limp, no uncomfortable Zander questions. My plan was to get Zander on a bike as fast as I could. This would allow him to see me as a normal dad. With this I could fulfil the role as an exciting, involved, and capable daddy.

Zander was able to ride a two-wheeler bike two months before he turned three. Once on the bike, I was able to take him out and play with him until he was completely worn out.

I remember one day the two of us headed out on the bikes. We cycled from my parents' house to the office in the Holy Loch Marina and then back to my parents - 12 miles, and with some hills on the way, and he was only three years old. But this was exactly what I had wanted to be able to do with him; to be a father who could do this type of thing with his son. Please note, at no stage was I pushing him; this was all his doing, and on this particular day I had to say: "That's enough now Zander, enough cycling for today buddy." It was him pushing me.

While I was out doing boys' stuff with Z, Sarah was being her usual 'fabulous mother' self. We both were playing very important roles in Zander's life, each in our own way. We both adored him, while being sure not to spoil him. He was a toddler who was showered with our time, love, and the lessons of life.

We were both loving life with Zander and we were doing all of it to the best of our ability. Admittedly, and I am sure this is the case with everyone and their first child, being parents at first was so daunting and you constantly question yourself about whether you're doing it right. It's not like you do a course about how to be a parent. But we knew when to rely on one another; we quickly discovered where our strengths as parents were.

Sarah had gone back to work. She had decided that working for herself was the best way to go. This was ideal; she could shape her day any way she needed it to be. Sarah really did deserve a medal, as I still required a lot of her time with my situation. There was also the situation with the chemo every three months. So Sarah was the one who kept things moving smoothly in our wee family's household. Not an easy thing to do - I was eating specific diets, taking injections, sometimes steroids, sometimes pain killers and all of this being kept well out the view of Z. We really didn't want him entering this part of my world and it becoming normality for him. As he has been getting older though and needed to go to the doctor for his inoculations, the timing came right for me to introduce him to me taking my daily injection. I was hoping it would help him feel more relaxed about getting his from the doctor.

Sarah, for many reasons, is my most valued and loyal friend. She has proved herself over and over again. She stayed at my side when I needed a crutch, is the most fabulous and dedicated mother that a father could ask for his child, and when the going gets tough she keeps calm, cool and collected.

Due to work and other areas of life, Sarah and I were spending more and more time apart. If I was working Sarah would have Z, and when she was working I would have Z. Don't get me wrong, we were quite happy with this, but as a couple we were just not getting the time a relationship should have and we were both accepting this. As parents though Z was certainly getting our time; we would insist on it without even thinking about it.

Something was becoming more obvious to both of us. It was a word coming up more and more. It was the word 'friend'. We had been through so much together - enough to write a book about! Now the way both of us viewed it, was that friends are very important, you need them, and if you're like me you will let them come very close to you. I do love and rely on my friends, but at our age and with what we had faced we both needed a wee bit more.

This was discussed over time and always very calmly. There was never any shouting and this calmness speaks volumes on its own. We had naturally progressed to having our own lives. We met fully 100 per cent when it involved Zander.

I would go to the office seven days a week back then. Working and growing your own business can be a 24 hour a day, seven days a week job, and more often than not three in the morning is when you do your paranoid, ridiculous thinking. I came into the house one day and Sarah gave me a letter to read.

I went through to the living room to read it. It was handwritten. She came in and sat on the couch next to me, like a good friend would. The two of us became upset while I read this very personal letter basically saying what I have just mentioned. It covered what we had discussed as partners the past wee while. We discussed it further. We spoke like adults, we spoke like friends. But the relationship had to change. No one was dumped, no one was cheated on, it was a mutual agreement. I thanked Sarah for writing the letter covering all that the two of us had touched on over the past while.

Zander was at an age where I could move out and it would not affect him too badly if we were careful, and we always would be. I moved into my late grandparents' house, 'Jacksonville', which I had bought from the family when my grandparents passed away. It was three hundred metres from where we were together at Maymor.

Zander knew Jacksonville too; it wasn't strange to him, as the two of us had walked around to it on a number of occasions. This did concern me at first - was being close possibly a danger? I had visions of Zander, who was now three years old, deciding to pop along and visit his Dad of his own accord and while doing so crossing two main roads. This was something that played on my mind. I had to look after Jacksonville though, and this was the reason we gave to Zander. He understood this. He only ever saw Sarah and I being respectful to one another and I was moving out to look after the house along the road. This was emotional, to say the least, but the situation was required all of us to make the most out of life.

I had popped in to see Zander on the way home to Jacksonville after work one day. This was not uncommon for me; I would pop in a good bit and have dinner maybe once a week with Zander and Sarah. I was sitting on the living room floor talking with Z. It was his dinner time. I said: "OK, I'm going to head back round to Jacksonville Z".

He came over for his kiss and cuddle goodbye and said: "Daddy do you not live here anymore with us?" I said, while giving him his cuddle goodbye: "I have to look after old Gran and Papa's house Z, you and Mum are looking after this house, and I am looking after Jacksonville."

He was happy with this. After giving him his kiss and cuddle goodbye I left. I got in the car and cried. I'm crying about it just now while writing. But Zander was happy with the explanation and it was never mentioned by him again. This was his normality. He has never been short of our love or attention and I think this is what is important. I travel a lot with work now and we have the wonderful gift of Skype. I can be on the other side of the world and still say goodnight to my boy as if I was there.

To this day, Sarah and I still rely on one another and not only for parenting Zander. She will always be my valuable friend, a friend who I'm lucky enough to have as my son's mother and who stood fast at my side when I needed her. Annette, her old boss, was right when she told me: "She is one of the most loyal committed people I know."

Chapter 40 – The Three Peaks Challenge

Ok, so right at the beginning of the book and from my first MS attack you will have heard me mention my aim of fighting back to doing the UK's 'Three Peaks Challenge'. This would involve climbing the three highest peaks in England, Wales and Scotland, often within 24 hours.

I kept this in my sights right from the start when I first found out that I was ill and had that first very aggressive attack late in 2005. I know it was late in 2005 because it was around my birthday and that's in October. The Three Peaks Challenge was constantly in my thoughts when I was teaching myself to walk again, back at my parent's hall when I was using their tiles as my markers and then when I progressed to the road in front of their house with the lampposts as part of my Fartlek training style.

I believe that when you want to get yourself somewhere in life then you must have a focus on it and already see yourself there; well, it certainly helps me, and I promise you that every single wee bit of help you can get does make the difference.

So, I was pushing out the distance when out walking along the Innellan road. The road runs directly alongside the Clyde, and it looks over to the Cloch Lighthouse, where the Clyde swim starts from.

To start with this walk was very hard going; not due to pain but more to do with my body. After a certain distance it would just not do as I asked it. However, the more frequently I drove myself and pushed myself to walk further and further down the Innellan road, I noticed the further I could go. Noticing things like this made - and still makes - the difference. I was now getting closer to covering the distance I needed to crack The Three Peaks.

I finally spoke to my loyal friends who had said they would do it with me. My friends were very much a vital part of this life-changing event.

The Three Peaks is exciting to the many people who choose to step up to it every year, but to me it was so much more than a physical challenge. To me it was proof that my theory, which until this point I had kept to myself, that the way I was dealing with this condition was not just a defence mechanism to stop me becoming depressed, but a real way to handle it.

People of perfect health need to train when running a marathon or taking on another physical challenge. I have to do the same - and then some! I must ignore the pain, the fatigue, and adjust to being insanely dizzy. From what I have experienced, I do all I can to make it my normality and then crack on. Admittedly, having to accept change for my theory to work plays a massive part.

I put it to a number of friends again to see who was keen. I had

17 friends and family who wanted to do it with me. I looked at what was required; the day with maximum daylight; the best sequence in which to climb the peaks; and obviously we needed a start point and a finish point. We also had to decide how best to utilise our 24 hours travelling from mountain to mountain.

We all lived in Scotland, so it made sense to finish there, so after getting off Ben Nevis we didn't have too far to drive to get home to bed. The added beauty was that on the final mountain you only have to get to the top in the 24 hours' time allowed, and Ben Nevis was the highest of them. Also, doing it in this order was going to be the shortest way. Once summited, the challenge, time-wise, was complete, and we could take our time coming down the mountain back to the mini bus and the drive home.

So I had my route and my team planned with Liam, the owner of Cairngorm Adventure Guides. He was a good friend of old, and a very capable and experienced mountain climber and leader and he agreed that the plan was a good one.

Everything made sense, and we picked Sunday June 21st as the date that suited all the requirements, of which there were quite a few, so this alone was a challenge.

I needed two mini buses so I spoke to Peter Wilson, head instructor at a local outdoor education centre in Toward. Peter and I had known of each other for many years, and we shared the same interests and had the same type of drive. I knew he would offer to help where he could; he always does, whether it is kayak safety support at the Clyde swim or use of his outdoor education centre's mini buses for the Three Peaks. Part of the joys of living in a small town such as Dunoon is that assistance is never too far away.

Finally June 20th arrived, and we made our way down to Wales where we were booked into a hostel to get a good night's sleep and an easy start for climbing Snowdon the following day. The plan was to kick off sharp in the morning and be at the foot of Snowdon for a 9.30am start to our Three Peaks Challenge.

We began on a high note, and it stayed with us for the rest of the experience. The weather was great; perfect for what we had ahead of us, dry but not too warm. We were making good ground going up Snowdon, and we met another team who seemed to share the same focus and drive. It turned out that we saw them on every other mountain during this time. Good effort lads, I assume you also made it.

We got off Snowdon and were on the road for 1.45pm and on the road heading towards Scafell Pike. It was a winding road on the approach to Scafell, but we got there in good time and ready to start at 5.45pm and finished 11.30pm and back in our trusty mini buses driven by Victor (Dad) and Adam (Clyde swimmer, and good friend). With little time to spare we were on the road and driving towards our final mountain, the mighty Ben Nevis.

We started 4.30am and summited 7.45am. I was in my own world just following the bloke in front. In my time I had become a well experienced hill walker but I knew I had nothing to add to the leadership which was in place. Liam is a very experienced and professional individual; he was leading this day for us and I knew I could relax.

You see, by this point I knew I had the required energy and drive to do this. But it would have become so much harder for me had there been a wrong turn or if we were required to back track so I was confident that the man at the front with the map was the right guy for us all to be following. As we were getting higher it was getting lighter and I knew the morning was coming.

Keeping an eye on our time I was happy that we were going to crack this. I was going to do this! It was about to be such a turning point for me living with MS. I could do physically tough stuff that my illness-free friends could do.

Finally we were at the top of Ben Nevis and we all shook hands and gave each other pats on the back. I was overwhelmed and speechless, which is unlike me. I was asked to say a few words and I wished I had planned something, but all I could muster up was a thanks and a 'let's get back to the car'. I knew though that the team all understood the significance of these 24 hours, but it meant so much more than I spoke of at the time. In fact, I possibly didn't even realise myself at the time.

the summit of Ben Nevis

Chapter 41 – Staying Positive

Well, here I am at the end of my book.

I think you will agree it's been one hell of a journey so far, with very high ups and certainly educational downs. I've enjoyed telling you my story and bringing you into my life at the safe distance of your own body. I wanted to share my story and exciting experiences with you and I hope you've found it both entertaining as well as educational.

I'm going to take you back to the beginning of the book, when I had just been told by my GP Glen that there were lesions on my brain that were likely causing me to have numb toes.

I walked out of Glen's surgery and went across the path to the wall that ran parallel to it. I slid down the wall and sat on the ground with my head in my hands experiencing a new level of panic.

Now looking back it is so clear to me that what I was experiencing is obviously a built-in safety mechanism. I'd like to share it with you because it is something that has taught me to walk twice in my adult life so far, and it's something that makes me able to smile and even laugh in the face of adversity.

Outside Glen's surgery I had become claustrophobic in my own body. Until that point, my body had been a place I had lived in with total comfort - actually in luxurious comfort. When it all went pear shaped for me I realised I am not my body; it's just where I live. It's not me - sure it's what I see when I look in the mirror; but for me to see it looking back the lights must be on, because If they're not, I cannot see it but I am aware of it.

I look back at my life before I became ill, and am quite at ease with the fact that I used my body back then to the max. So I would like to leave a thought with you to nurture.

If doctors were to turn to me and say: "Paul, we have a new body for you", I would take it in a second, not caring a jot about its past religion or race. I would just be thankful for, well, for a working body. I would then take my second chance with my new fully functional body and I would use it to the max in every way I could. I would make the world my gym again, and have no limits whatsoever, but now I would be more productive in the world - not that I wasn't before, but I had concerns and worries when there really was nothing to worry about.

But for the time being, until medical science makes those advances, I will continue to attack life with the same ferocity, tenacity and stubbornness, using what I've learned about morals and karma in the recent years.

Before I became ill, I admit my life was all about me. What excitement can PK make for himself today? But since having Zander, and living with my health situation, I have learned that life is not about 'me' but actually all about 'we', us, the world. What can I do for others now? I'm still the same guy with never-ending mental energy and motivation. At the start I considered myself trapped in my circumstances, but now I am in a completely relaxed state where I don't let pointless worries enter my life. I make my choices matter.

Whatever the future may have in store, my health as a person is not a concern for me. Of course I do think about how it might affect the people closest to me. But I make a conscious effort not to become wrapped up in my own situation because I firmly believe thoughts become things, good and bad.

If you have a worry, whether it is pressure from the bank about a debt, or if you are getting fat, then I don't think it helps to elevate the problem by putting all your negative thoughts and worry, in effect putting all your powerful energies into the problem.

What works for me is visualising myself in the worry-free place without these problems and in a life free of care. Think about it; it makes no sense when wishing to get rid of a problem to put all your mental energy and thought into the problem. Surely focusing on the solution, or even thinking, 'it might never even happen', and putting your energy into how that feels, is more productive than applying it to the actual worry? You can train yourself to think like this and I promise you will be amazed how life-changing it can be.

The main thing I can pass on to you though is - we are not our bodies, we just live in them - so be happy in yourself now, and don't wait for something tragic to happen before you wake up to this fact. You owe it to yourself to enjoy and use what you have to the max.

Thank you for giving my story your priceless and precious time.

Paul Kerr

2015

Lightning Source UK Ltd.
Milton Keynes UK
UKHW021019200820
368550UK00018B/2146